E CAPTAIN'S TABLE

BRYAN ROBSON Column

I'VE now been an England player for more than eight years and I don't think I've ever been part of a better international team than the one which Bobby Robson has at the moment.

In fact I would go so far as to say that today's England team is almost as good as those famous World Cup winners of 1966.

I can't even begin to describe what a tremendous pride and thrill I take in leading my country out of Wembley. I'm a patriotic person who believes it is very important for us to have a strong representative team in our national sport.

Nobody was more disappointed than me when we failed to qualify for the 1984 European Championship Finals and I vowed then not to miss out on any more major international tournaments.

So far I've been able to keep that promise, and now I'm looking to be in Italy for the next World Cup Finals in 1990.

We're in a very tough qualifying group with Sweden, Poland and Albania, so getting to the Finals is not going to be as easy as some of our supporters seem to think.

The Swedes are a particularly strong team at the moment and comparisons with the Danish team of a few years ago are not an exaggeration.

Poland are no pushovers, either, and against Albania we really are stepping into the unknown.

But I'm nevertheless confident that this England team can finish top of the pile and go on to make a very big impression in the Finals.

Jack Charlton said recently that the 1966 England team had five world class players. He went on to point out that Bobby Robson's current team has six or seven men who come into that category.

The player he had the greatest praise for was Gary Lineker, and I would agree

One of England's greatest talents—Liverpool winger John Barnes.

£3.50

THE CAPTAIN'S ABLE

that Gary is the deadliest finisher in the world at present.

Because they don't always play to his strengths at Barcelona, Gary has not scored as many goals as he is capable of at club level in the last year or so. But he is on target virtually every time he pulls on an England shirt, and that is because we know the best way to utilise Gary's incredible pace and uncanny knack of being in the right place at the right time.

The man who takes greatest credit for that has to be Peter Beardsley, who is now starting to receive the credit for the brilliant job he has been doing for the past three years.

People have criticised Peter for not scoring enough goals, but they have to realise that if he started getting more selfish in front of goal, Gary Lineker's strike rate would suffer as a result.

We all take the mickey out of Peter for the number of times he's passed up a virtual certain opening to allow Gary to score. But there's a lot of games we wouldn't have won without that selfless attitude.

One man who appreciates the brilliant job Peter does is his Liverpool boss Kenny Dalglish. He knew that if he was

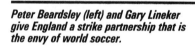

Peter Beardsley (left) and Gary Lineker give England a strike partnership that is the envy of world soccer.

going to replace Ian Rush, then he'd need someone to lay on the chances for John Aldridge. It cost him a British record £1.9 million to get Peter, but it was money well spent.

An even better Liverpool bargain has proved to be John Barnes, who now has the soccer world at his feet following 18 incredible months at Anfield.

There was never any question mark against John's ability when he was a Watford player, but there were doubts about his consistency.

Wherever England go in the world, there is always someone who still wants to talk to John about his fantastic goal

against the Brazilians in 1984.

But that goal has become like a millstone around John's neck until his move to Anfield because he was expected to make runs like that every time he got the ball.

No disrespect to Watford, but when he was at Vicarage Road John often had to do everything on his own up front.

At Liverpool, he is surrounded by world class players who can take the ball off him when he needed a breather. As a result, he is now turning in match winning performances week after week.

Add to those players the names of Peter Shilton, Terry Butcher and Kenny

Sansom and you can maybe begin to understand why England are facing the future with such optimism.

And even though much has been made of the fact that I'm now approaching my 32nd birthday, I also intend to play my part.

I am still capable of playing my usual midfield role, but if Bobby Robson feels it is time for us to start thinking about a sweeper, I'll be happy to fill that job.

If it will prolong my international career, I'd even be prepared to play in goal. But I think Chris Woods might have something to say about that one. After waiting so many years for Shilts to show his age, the last thing he needs is for someone else to join the queue!

Bryan Robson.

SALUTE THE CHAMPIONS

KENNY DALGLISH'S red army swept all before them as they marched relentlessly on in the most one-sided Championship race for years.

And, before Liverpool had reached the FA Cup Final, every superlative was exhausted in order to pay fitting tribute to the most successful English club in history.

In the eyes of many, this current Liverpool side is the cream of a crop of brilliant teams born out of Anfield. There is certainly no one to touch them for consistency at the moment.

The side is young enough, and the squad strong enough, to keep Liverpool at the top of the tree and according to skipper Alan Hansen "we are going to get even better."

Not only did they win a memorable League Championship for an amazing 17th time, they also swept the board in terms of individual honours with John Barnes winning both the PFA and the Football Writers' Player of the Year awards.

Kenny Dalglish inevitably picked up the Bells Manager of the Year award. The Reds missed out on the Littlewoods and FA Cup, but are probably saving that for this season.

Ronnie Whelan, John Barnes and Craig Johnston had plenty to celebrate last season.

LIVERPOOL'S ROUTE TO THE CHAMPIONSHIP

Date	Opponent	Score	Scorers
Aug 15	Arsenal (a)	2-1	(Aldridge, Nicol)
Aug 29	Coventry (a)	4-1	(Nicol 2, Aldridge pen, Beardsley)
Sep 5	West Ham (a)	1-1	(Aldridge pen)
Sep 12	Oxford (h)	2-0	(Aldridge, Barnes)
Sep 15	Charlton (h)	3-2	(Aldridge pen, Hansen, McMahon)
Sep 20	Newcastle (a)	1-0	(Nicol 3, Aldridge)
Sep 29	Derby (h)	4-0	(Aldridge 2 pens, Beardsley)
Oct 3	Portsmouth (h)	4-0	(Beardsley, McMahon, Aldridge pen, Whelan)
Oct 17	QPR (h)	4-0	(Johnston, Aldridge pen, Barnes 2)
Oct 24	Luton (a)	1-0	(Gillespie)
Nov 1	Everton (h)	2-0	(McMahon, Beardsley)
Nov 4	Wimbledon (a)	1-1	(Houghton)
Nov 15	Man. United (a)	1-1	(Aldridge)
Nov 21	Norwich (h)	0-0	
Nov 24	Watford (h)	4-0	(McMahon, Houghton, Aldridge, Barnes)
Nov 28	Tottenham (a)	2-0	(McMahon, Johnston)
Dec 6	Chelsea (h)	2-1	(Aldridge pen, McMahon)
Dec 11	S'thampton (a)	2-2	(Barnes 2)
Dec 19	Sheff. Wed. (h)	1-0	(Gillespie)
Dec 26	Oxford (a)	3-0	(Aldridge, Barnes, McMahon)
Dec 28	Newcastle (h)	4-0	(McMahon, Aldridge 2, 1 pen, Houghton)
Jan 1	Coventry (h)	4-0	(Beardsley 2, Aldridge, Houghton)
Jan 16	Arsenal (h)	2-0	(Aldridge, Beardsley)
Jan 23	Charlton (a)	2-0	(Beardsley, Barnes)
Feb 6	West Ham (h)	0-0	
Feb 13	Watford (a)	4-1	(Beardsley 2, Aldridge, Barnes)
Feb 27	Portsmouth (a)	2-0	(Barnes 2)
Mar 5	QPR (a)	1-0	(Barnes)
Mar 16	Derby (a)	1-1	(Johnston)
Mar 20	Everton (a)	0-1	
Mar 26	Wimbledon (h)	2-1	(Aldridge, Barnes)
Apr 2	Nott'm For. (a)	1-2	(Aldridge pen)
Apr 4	Man. United (h)	3-3	(Beardsley, Gillespie, McMahon)
Apr 13	Nott'm For. (h)	5-0	(Houghton, Aldridge 2, Gillespie, Beardsley)
Apr 20	Norwich (a)	0-0	
Apr 23	Tottenham (h)	1-0	(Beardsley)
Apr 30	Chelsea (a)	1-1	(Barnes)
May 2	S'thampton (h)	1-1	(Aldridge)
May 7	Sheff. Wed (a)	5-1	Johnston 2, Barnes 1, Beardsley 2
May 9	Luton (h)	1-1	Aldridge

LEADING SCORERS

John Aldridge 26
John Barnes 15
Peter Beardsley 15
Steve McMahon 9

THE ROAD TO WEMBLEY

3rd Round	Stoke (a)	0-0
3rd Round replay	Stoke (h)	1-0 (Beardsley)
4th Round	Aston Villa (a)	2-0 (Barnes, Beardsley)
5th Round	Everton (a)	1-0 (Houghton)
6th Round	Man. City (a)	4-0 (Houghton, Beardsley pen, Johnston, Barnes)
Semi-Final	Nott'm Forest	2-1 (Aldridge 2, 1 pen)
Final	Wimbledon	0-1

LEADING SCORERS

Peter Beardsley 3
John Aldridge 2
John Barnes 2
Ray Houghton 2
Craig Johnston 1

JOHN BAR

England's great entertainer

I JOINED Liverpool because I wanted to win things, but the events of my first season at Anfield exceeded my greatest expectations.

To have lifted the PFA Award as well as the Footballer of the Year trophy was simply unbelievable.

After from losing to Everton in the Littlewoods Cup, which was no disgrace anyway, and missing the game which decided the title through injury, it was success all the way.

Although my £900,000 transfer from Watford last summer didn't

present any fears, despite the fact I'd kept Liverpool hanging around for my signature and the fans were maybe a little sceptical, I did feel a certain curiosity as to how I would fit into the Anfield system.

But I can honestly say that I didn't have any problems on that score and I settled into the side

quicker than I anticipated.

The thing to remember, though, is that I'd already played in about ten friendlies for Liverpool before the season kicked off so it wasn't as if I was going in cold.

By that time I felt part of the set-up and my early success can be put down to the fact I had so many quality players around me, rather than my own individual performances. Playing alongside people like Peter Beardsley and Steve McMahon would make anyone look good.

RNES
eat

Having said that, however, I was very pleased with my own contribution throughout the season and I'd like to think I've gone some way towards proving that I can be consistent.

Virtually throughout my Watford career the critics claimed I was inconsistent and that was obviously something I was keen to put right when I signed for Liverpool. Hopefully I've seen the last of those stories.

The fact there are so many quality players in reserve at Anfield encourages you to be consistent because you are well aware that a couple of below-par performances could cost you your place.

And, while Peter Beardsley and I were the two most expensive players in the team, even we weren't safe from the axe. No one is at Liverpool and that's one of the reasons why the club has been so successful over the years.

It was also important for me to maintain a high performance level throughout the season in order to keep my place in the England squad and hopefully produce my club form on an international stage.

Consistency is the key to success in this game and no-one has mastered that better than Liverpool. The difference between Liverpool and the rest is that while some teams can live with us over 90 minutes, there aren't many who can do it over a whole season.

Struggled

Everton beat us twice last season, Manchester United held us in both League games and Forest also gave us a run for our money but all three struggled to compete with us on a long-term basis.

The fact that four Liverpool players – myself, Steve McMahon, Peter Beardsley and skipper Alan Hansen – occupied the top four places in the Player of the Year honours list spoke volumes for our domination.

And I agree with our captain when he says that we are going to get even better.

Billy McMystery

Billy McNeill has proved to be a brilliant manager with both Aberdeen and Celtic. So why was he such a failure at Manchester City and Aston Villa?
MICHAEL GRAHAM,
DRUMCHAPEL.

I don't know all the background to what went on at Maine Road and Villa Park. Maybe he just developed an allergy to the English air. He was very lucky to land the Celtic job after his dismal time down South, particularly as David Hay had done nothing to merit the sack.

But having landed on his feet, Billy has made the most of his opportunity. His dealings in the transfer market have been excellent. And it has been a remarkable achievement to put Rangers in the shade when you consider the spending power which Graeme Souness has been able to enjoy.

Vinny Jones might be a hard man but he's not cunning with it.

JUST JIM

Mad Vinny

How much longer is Wimbledon's Vinny Jones going to get away with his blatant strong-arm tactics? It's about time he was called to order.
CARL GRIFFITHS,
LEATHERHEAD, SURREY.

Vinny's career certainly hasn't been helped by all the controversy he's generated. But in terms of the hard men, he's nowhere near top of the league. Vinny may get in some wicked challenges, but at least he isn't sneaky about it. The really effective hatchet men are those players who give you a good kick without anyone else seeing it. Jones commits every foul right under the referee's nose. That's why he's always in trouble. But others commit far worse fouls and get away with them.

Foreign flops

Why do our top stars continue to sign for European clubs when even players of the quality of Ian Rush and Gary Lineker have failed to fit into the Continental system?
SALLY HENDERSON,
WASHINGTON, TYNE & WEAR.

They go for one reason only – MONEY. Anyone who claims they're crossing the Channel "for the challenge" is speaking with forked tongue. I joined Inter Milan simply because they offered me more money than Chelsea could pay me. But I hated it out there and as soon as the maximum wage rule was lifted I was back like a shot. Signing for a foreign club involves a lot more hassles than today's players seem to bargain for.

Second class City

Manchester City have not stopped talking about their brilliant youngsters for the past two years, yet they're still in the Second Division. How much longer must we wait for them to make it back to the big time?
TERRY McLEAN,
BUXTON, DERBYS.

I hope they win promotion this season because a club with the resources and support of City should be in the First Division. I can't help feeling they're suffering from a superiority complex. It's time they stopped talking about how great their players are and set about proving it.

8

JIMMY GREAVES dips into his postbag and answers some of your letters. Just Jim appears in SHOOT every week with £10 paid to the best letter and £5 for all others published. Send your letters to: Just Jim, SHOOT Magazine, King's Reach Tower, Stamford Street, London SE1 9LS.

Sack Robson

England should sack Bobby Robson and appoint Brian Clough as manager. We all know Cloughie is the man to lead us to World Cup glory.

TERRY NEWCOMBE,
CREWE, CHESHIRE.

Speak for yourself, pal. As far as I'm concerned Robson has been the best England boss since Alf Ramsey, who won the World Cup and a Knighthood. I don't know who will get the thankless task of eventually replacing Bobby, but I do know that it won't be Cloughie. I'm possibly Brian's biggest fan, but even I know he'll never get the nod from Lancaster Gate. The England manager has to be a real diplomat wherever he travels. Cloughie would probably start World War Three within two weeks.

Scouser Saint

Will UEFA's ruling that Scotsmen are now officially classed as foreigners affect the running of the Saint and Greavsie?

MARTIN MURRAY,
SKEGNESS, LINCS.

Of course it will. From now on, 70 per cent of the show's presenters must be English, so the Saint has to become one fifth English. I suggested we replace his head with an English one which talks sense, but because he's lived in the Anfield boot room for 20 years he claims he's now a naturalised scouser.

Top Spur

My dad, who is a Tottenham fanatic, says you were the greatest player he's ever seen at White Hart Lane. Who do you consider Tottenham's all-time best?

GRAHAM ROSS,
ISLINGTON, LONDON N1.

Dave Mackay. The man was a soccer genius. Everyone remembers him as the man who never shirked a tackle in the middle of the park, and there's no denying that I was glad Dave was on my side. But he wasn't just a destroyer. Dave was a fantastic captain who made everyone believe he was a world beater. He also possessed incredible vision and a tremendous pass.

Welsh woe

Why is it that Northern Ireland and Eire can both qualify for major Finals while the Welsh, with arguably better players, always miss out?

COLIN POWELL,
NEWPORT, GWENT.

Because the Welsh FA couldn't organise a 'drink up' in a brewery and as soon as any Welsh team looks like gaining some degree of success they stick their oar in and cock it all up. Even now I still don't know why Mike England was sacked and until the manager is allowed to run his team without interference from above, the Welsh will continue to struggle.

Arsenal attack

Why are you always having a go at Arsenal? Is it because you used to play for Tottenham that you hate The Gunners so much?

NICKY ANASTASI,
KILBURN, LONDON NW7

I don't hate Arsenal. In fact, I've got a lot of time for George Graham and think some of the youngsters he's grooming at Highbury can become big stars in the next few years. I admire George for refusing to be held to ransom in the transfer market. But when all his Championship rivals are spending money like it's going out of fashion, then he has no alternative but to compete if he wants success.

Allen out

Has Clive Allen wrecked his England career by leaving Spurs for French club Bordeaux?

JOHN TRACY,
ANDOVER, HANTS.

He wasn't exactly an international regular before his move, and I think he realised that when he agreed to the deal. But if Bobby Robson's comments about the standard of the French League are anything to go by, Clive certainly hasn't improved his chances of an England recall.

Bobby Robson has done an excellent job as boss of England.

KICK-QU

Pat Bonner is an international for who? (See Q. 1).

1 Celtic goalkeeper Pat Bonner is capped at international level by which country?

2 Which Third Division club did Andy Jones leave to join Charlton at the start of the 1987–88 season?

3 There are two teams in the Football League in which the letter A appears three times. Who are they?

4 Leeds Utd tough tackling defender Noel Blake (left) is a full England international. Is the statement true or false?

What is Paul Goddard's nickname and when was Steve McMahon's England debut? (See Q. 8 and 12).

OFF

Continued on page 66

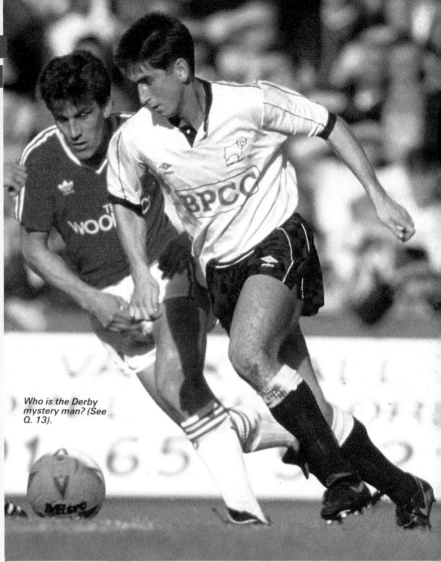

Who is the Derby mystery man? (See Q. 13).

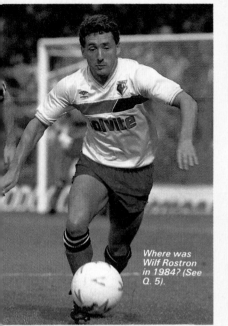

Where was Wilf Rostron in 1984? (See Q. 5).

Gary Mackay had a scoring Scotland debut against who? (See Q. 17).

5 Why did Watford skipper Wilf Rostron miss the club's 1984 FA Cup Final defeat by Everton?

6 The Hornets met The Tigers in a FA Cup Third Round tie last season. Who were the two teams involved?

7 Diego Maradona has played for Argentinos Juniors, Barcelona, Naples and which other League club?

8 Is striker Paul Goddard nicknamed, Sarge, Captain or Major?

9 Who did Graeme Souness buy from St. Mirren last season for a £1 million transfer fee?

10 Name the four other countries that were in the Republic of Ireland's 1988 European Championship qualifying group?

11 Manchester United's Steve Bruce joined the club from Norwich. Which other League club has he played for?

12 Who were the opposition when Steve McMahon made his international debut for England last season?

13 Do you know the name of the Derby winger pictured in action against Charlton (above)?

14 Apart from being on the winning side, what have Glenn Hoddle and Arnold Muhren in common in FA Cup Finals?

15 Can you name the two brothers who helped Luton to Cup glory last season?

16 Can you identify the England defender who was born in Singapore and nearly died after breaking his nose?

17 Hearts midfielder Gary Mackay scored the winner on his Scotland debut against which country in 1987?

18 Which Middlesbrough defender made his England debut against Hungary in a 0-0 draw last season?

19 Trevor Hebberd scored the first goal for who against QPR in the Littlewoods Cup Final in 1986?

20 Which former England striker is currently in charge of Second Division Oldham?

11

IT'S TOUG

WHEN Billy Bonds first came into the world of football you could buy a family house for under £3,000, have a pint of beer for the equivalent of 6p and get a brand new bicycle for £20!

Now that after-match pint is over a pound, a similar house in Bonzo-land in South-East London is about £80,000–£100,000, and most boys know that you won't get much more than a bicycle wheel for £20.

A lot has changed on and off the pitch since 15-year-old Billy walked into the Valley to join Charlton (they don't even play at the same ground any more for starters) as a ground staff boy back in May 1962, doubling up as an apprentice fitter in a factory.

Elvis Presley and Frank Ifield were riding high in the charts and England were about to go out to eventual winners Brazil in the Quarter-Finals of the World Cup in Chile.

The young Billy would not have watched it on his own telly – a black-and-white one (no colour then) would have set him back £90, more than one would cost today!

"It was a few years ago," admits Bonds, now 42, "and a few things have changed."

The basic tools of the trade – the ball, boots and even pitches – certainly have.

"Nowadays you can wear a brand new pair of boots and, if you soak them in water or add a little vaseline, there are no ill-effects. When I first started playing you had to play several practice games to wear them in.

"Balls were much heavier and still had the lacing on them but at least all the pitches were grass. I can't stand plastic pitches.

Graduates

"I think they are absolutely useless and should all be taken up."

By the time Billy graduated from giving out the Horlicks in the dressing-room to the Charlton first team the Kinks' "You Really Got Me" was number one and the England cricket team was preparing to go on tour to South Africa.

It was a very different Football League that Bonds broke into in the 1964–65 season. He made his Second Division debut against a Northampton side that won promotion to the First at the end of the campaign.

Fulham, Burnley and Wolves were in that First Division, Oxford in the Fourth, Wimbledon and Hereford won promotion to the Southern League (now Beazer Homes League), Premier Division that season while in Scotland, Kilmarnock won the title with Rangers fifth and Celtic eighth – below Clyde!

"I'd agree with Bob Paisley's view

HER!

that there were more good sides around then, although Liverpool have been the team to beat ever since I arrived at West Ham,'' says Bonds who came to Upton Park in May 1967 for £45,000.

"However teams are better organised these days, especially the weaker international sides. The consequences, though, are less goals, less goal-mouth incidents and fewer exciting games.

"The game has got a lot quicker and harder – we do do more work on the physical side than we used to in training.''

When Bonds moved across the Thames to West Ham, 'flower power' was on the rise, Scott McKenzie topped the charts exhorting people to wear flowers in their hair en route to San Francisco and The Beatles released 'Sergeant Pepper'.

Fashions

Times have certainly changed since Bonzo began on the road to soccer stardom.

Kit fashions have gone from the round collar and cuffs, to the wing collar and motif, through striped/diamonded arms to current V-neck and shadow-diamond or pin-stripe effect.

"It seems to change with fashions,'' says Bonds. "There isn't much difference in the quality though, I suppose it'll be back to baggy shorts one day.''

Billy's appearance has changed over the years as well.

One of the other biggest changes for players is that they now travel to matches by luxury coach rather than by train.

"Coaches are more convenient, especially now they have coffee, toilets and videos,'' says Bonds. "You can get straight on at home, on to the motorway and get off at the ground the other end, instead of messing about at stations.''

We didn't like to ask Battling Billy if they were steam trains when he started.

Billy hated playing on plastic at QPR. Thankfully they've laid a new surface at Loftus Road.

PETER -THE

LIVERPOOL fans have paid homage to a myriad of talent down the years but, even by the club's remarkable standards, they have witnessed something extra special at Anfield this season.

The telepathic understanding and devastating brilliance of Peter Beardsley and John Barnes have taken the Merseyside giants into yet another memorable era.

Just as Hunt and St. John terrorised defences in the 60s and Keegan and Toshack did likewise in the 70s, so Beardsley and Barnes are tormenting opponents in the 80s with a blend of trickery and team-work unrivalled anywhere in Europe.

GREAT CREATOR

Gary Lineker has formed a superb partnership with Beardsley in the England side.

"If only one of us had joined Liverpool at the start of the season it could have been a different story because all eyes would have been on that one player. I'm the first to appreciate the role Peter has played in my settling in so well."

Time after time the two England stars combined with devastating effect down the Liverpool left, tearing even the best defences apart with their tireless running off the ball and setting up chance after chance for John Aldridge.

Yet while opponents were doubtless aware that, nine times out of ten, Barnes would find Beardsley in space – and vice-versa – they seemed powerless to resist their unique Merseyside magic.

"It's not something we work on but it just seems that when I'm in possession Peter always makes himself available," says Barnes. "If you're in trouble you can rely on him to get you out of it.

"You can't help but enjoy playing alongside him because, apart from the wide range of skills he possesses, he just never stops working and he's always likely to make something happen.

"I can't praise him highly enough and he deserves as much credit as anyone for me being named Player of the Year. Although he didn't settle in at Anfield as quickly as me, his presence was vital.

Memorable

"From Christmas until the end of the season he was our best player and in that memorable 5-0 League win over Nottingham Forest towards the end of the season he was out of this world."

Although Liverpool boss Kenny Dalglish refuses to single out individuals he too is full of admiration for the man he paid a British record £1.9 million to take over his own number seven shirt. Beardsley has more than justified the price tag . . . and the manager's sacrifice.

Because of the way Liverpool dominated and destroyed so many teams last term, goalkeeper Bruce Grobbelaar was redundant for much of the time. Not that he minded because it gave him chance to sit back and admire the wonderful work of his team-mates.

The performances of Beardsley and Barnes never cease to amaze the Zimbabwe-born keeper who says: "If the lads want a breather at all we just give either of them the ball.

"They combine so well and were so often the match winners for Liverpool last season.

"They rip people apart down the left where teams simply cannot cope with

The relationship they have forged during another all-conquering Liverpool season is not only good for club but for country as well and Bobby Robson must be grateful to Kenny Dalglish for bringing two England greats together.

But while supporters of Liverpool and England alike are currently singing the praises of Anfield disciples Peter and John, it wasn't so long ago that their seemingly unholy alliance was being branded a non-starter.

With Ian Rush gone, faint cries of discontent, among the red contingent of Merseyside at least, could be heard as

some questioned the arrival of such unashamed individual talent at a club whose previous success had been built on team-work and shared responsibilities.

But after a season which has seen Kenny Dalglish take Liverpool to even greater heights those doubts no longer exist.

Beardsley and Barnes have learned to complement their personal skills with the sort of unselfishness and awareness only Liverpool could have instilled. Each player is quick to praise the other and Barnes points out: "We have taken pressure off each other all season and that's had a lot to do with our success.

Continued overleaf

15

them. Although Peter is a great individual player, his talent lies in the way he blends in with the rest of the team.

"He is a dedicated team man, always working for the men around him. Some of the youngsters in the game who fancy themselves should notice the way he never stops running and working. He will do anything for the team."

If Beardsley had settled into the Liverpool side quicker than he did at the start of last season there's every chance he would have been named PFA Player of the Year instead of team-mate Barnes.

It took him at least ten games to begin to produce the form which persuaded Kenny Dalglish to splash out such a massive fee, by which time Barnes had established a substantial lead in the race for the game's top individual prize.

Beardsley in fact finished in third place behind team-mate Steve McMahon but ahead of skipper Alan Hansen – a result which underlined Liverpool's domination last season.

The former Newcastle idol is now a key figure for his country as well as his club but, despite being Britain's most expensive footballer, he insists: "I cannot agree with those who rate me an automatic choice for England.

"My point is that there is always someone coming through with eyes on your place in the side. Look at the way Neil Webb has emerged over the last season."

While Beardsley's performances for England – have always been whole-hearted – and at times brilliant – forming a tremendous partnership with Gary Lineker – his goal return is considered poor. He remains unconcerned, however.

"My only concern when I pull on an England shirt is to play my part in a victory. Winning is always what counts above all else at this level. I'm quite happy for Gary to grab all the goals.

"On the domestic front I was delighted to play my part in a memorable Liverpool season and I'm already looking forward to not only retaining the title, but adding the FA Cup to our honour's list this season."

Neil Webb has made tremendous progress for England over the past year.

John Aldridge has benefited from the arrival at Liverpool of John Barnes and Peter Beardsley.

Newcastle defender Peter Jackson and Sheffield Wednesday midfielder Gary Megson do battle in United's 1-0 victory at Hillsborough last season. Both sides experienced a mediocre time last term and will be looking for a major inprovement.

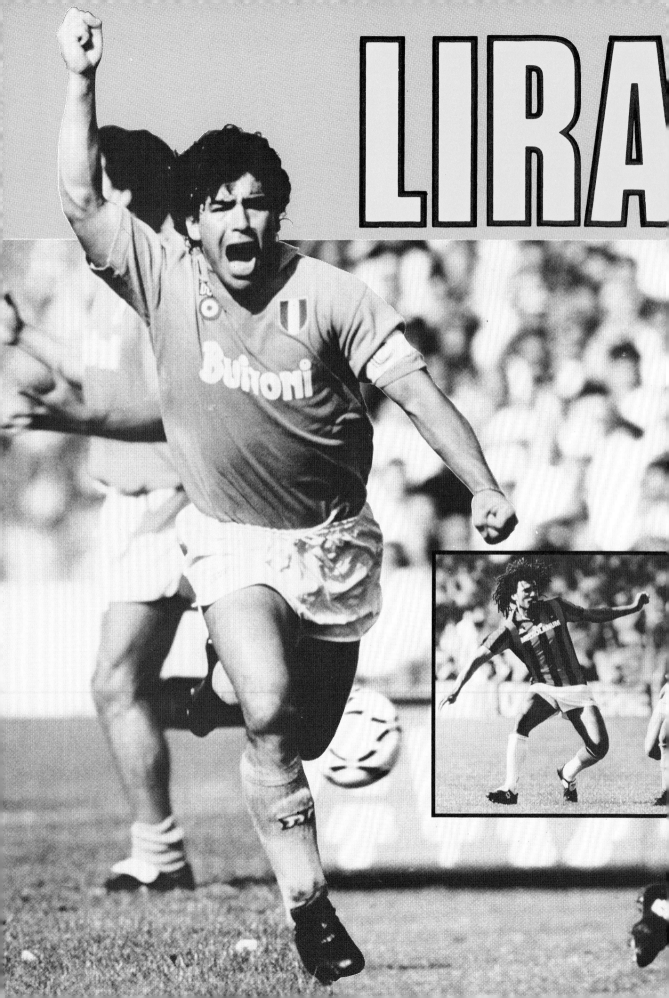

LIRA

MANIA

THE two most gifted footballers in the world head the battle for supremacy in the lira laden millionaire land of Italian soccer.

Diego Maradona inspired his Napoli side to their first Championship success in the 1986–87 season but even the little Argentinian couldn't prevent Rudi Gullit leading AC Milan to title glory last season.

Gullit cost the club over £5 million in 1987 when he joined them from PSV Eindhoven but it has proved a shrewd investment with the Dutchman's flowing locks, pop star image and tantalising skills making him a hero with the fans.

His strength, power in the air and subtle touch has, in many people's eyes, put him above Maradona in the quality stakes. Both are valued in the £10 million bracket and their high transfer fees are setting the trend in a country where football success is paramount.

Clubs are now forking out unbelievable sums to capture the top talents from around the world. Juventus spent £3·2 million strengthening their attack with the signing of Ian Rush. Inter bought West German international Lothar Matthaus from Bayern Munich for £2 million after splashing out on Belgium's Enzo Scifo and a host of other top sides are handing out the lira in their bid to topple the Gullit and Maradona show.

6 HITS

Shoot spotlight on the best buys of the 1987/88 season

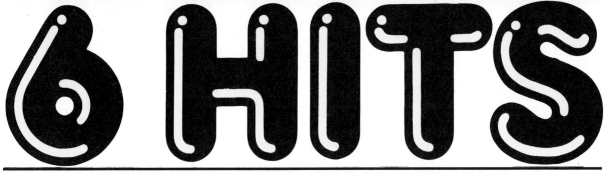

1 John Barnes (Liverpool)

AS the first black player of note to don the red of Liverpool there were fears that Barnes would not be accepted on Merseyside – but the England star became an instant hit and was soon hailed the new King of the Kop.

Manager Kenny Dalglish must be delighted with his £900,000 investment because, by the end of his first season at Anfield, the double Player of the Year had shot into the £2 million bracket.

2 Peter Beardsley (Liverpool)

DESPITE carrying the tag of Britain's most expensive footballer, the former Newcastle player has proved to be worth every penny of the £1.9 million Liverpool gambled on him.

Although it took him a few games to adapt to the Liverpool style Beardsley has been nothing short of a revelation, linking up in devastating fashion with England colleague John Barnes.

3 Brian McClair (Man United)

THE laid back Scot ignored all the pressure put on him by Press and public to break Manchester United's 20-goal hoodoo and prove himself a snip at £850,000.

The tribunal's valuation of the prolific former Celtic player, who still insists he's no goalscorer, seemed way off the mark a year ago. He has since made complete nonsense of the fee.

4 Michael O'Neill (Newcastle)

HIS arrival on Tyneside from Irish club Coleraine hardly caused the euphoria which followed the capture of Samba superstar Mirandinha, but O'Neill (above) didn't take long to put his Brazilian team-mate in the shade.

The 18-year-old Irishman made a mockery of his £80,000 fee by rattling in goals left, right and centre to keep Newcastle in the First Division.

5 Kevin Richardson (Arsenal)

THE no-nonsense midfielder slipped into The Gunners midfield with the minimum fuss, but maximum effect – much to the delight and relief of manager George Graham.

The Arsenal chief's £250,000 outlay has already been recouped with the former Watford and Everton battler (left) adding much-needed experience to a young side.

6 Paul Parker (QPR)

HIS move across London from Craven Cottage to Loftus Road may not have attracted the attention of some of last summer's big-money deals, but in the eyes of the QPR faithful Parker has been every much a hit as Barnes or Beardsley.

Despite his lack of inches the former England Under-21 international has proved you don't have to be a giant to be a central defender. A steal at £150,000.

McSTAY

IF fans in Scotland had to vote for one player destined for greatness, Celtic midfielder Paul McStay would probably win by a landslide.

While the whole country is rating him the near-equal of the legendary Jim Baxter, ONE man claims that far from reaching world class status, McStay has just served his APPRENTICESHIP.

"No way can I be compared to the great Jim Baxter (shown scoring a penalty against England in 1963)," says Mc Stay.

CONFESSES

I'm not a great player

"I must prove myself at international level for Scotland."

And that man is – current Player of the Year Paul McStay!

"It's plain daft comparing me with Baxter," says Paul. "I mean, he did it ALL for Rangers and Scotland in the Sixties, didn't he?

"Anyone who can SIT on the ball while playing for Scotland against England at Wembley is in a League of his own. The thought terrifies me!

"Sure, it's very flattering to be compared with really great players. And all the praise has done my confidence no harm at all. But what everyone must remember is I'm only 24-years old. It's still all in front of me – my BEST, that is!"

It's this claim that must make Celtic boss Billy McNeill a happy man now that he's got Paul fixed up on a new long-term contract. Particularly when the player admits he felt at the crossroads of his career at the end of the 1986–87 season.

"I felt I just wasn't heading in the right direction. I wasn't happy with my consistency and suffered a bit from the 'poor me's'. I suppose criticism rattled me too – especially if I knew it was right!

"The then manager David Hay did his best to lift my spirits but I wasn't sorry when the season ended. It was then I did some serious soul-searching.

Learning my trade

"I suddenly realised I had only been learning my trade. I had only been at Parkhead for four seasons and was therefore just beginning to mature.

"So I was able to shrug aside the accusation in some quarters that Celtic only played well when I played well. As far as I was concerned, it was now all about gaining experience."

Billy McNeill introduced new players last season which undoubtedly helped Paul in the fresh approach to his career at Parkhead. And he agrees that a lot of self-imposed responsibility has been lifted from his shoulders.

"There's a great buzz about the place now. The dressing-room is full of highly experienced players who probably have all gone through my old frame of mind. Every game is now a fresh challenge – not just a fixture to be fulfilled. Obviously teams are out to beat us now after last season's double triumph, but we've got a great side now.

"I'm hoping to be actively involved in the hectic international spell coming up for that will help to keep me sharp. Really, it's just like having a new lease of life. And there's plenty of room for improvement in my game.

"For instance, I want to score more goals from midfield and work on new ways of getting away from men detailed to mark me."

All of which must come as the worst possible news for every other team in the Premier Division.

SMASH HITS

Football's top of the pops

NINETEEN years ago, England the defending World Cup Champions lost their title, but marked the beginnings of an invasion of the pop singles chart.

On May 16th, 1970, the England World Cup Squad reached the number one position with their song 'Back Home', where it remained for three weeks. Amazing that the writers, Bill Martin and Phil Coulter, are both Scottish!

England also charted in 1982 with 'This Time' which faltered at number two, and again in 1986 with 'We've Got The Whole World At Our Feet' which peaked at a miserable 66.

They did better with their 1988 European Championship release "All the Way".

The Scottish World Cup Squads of 1974 and 1982 also scored hits. First with 'Easy Easy', and then with 'We Have A Dream'.

Many League clubs have charted on just one occasion. Among them are: Chelsea, with 'Blue Is The Colour' in 1972, which reached number five; Leeds, also in 1972, reached number ten with the self-titled 'Leeds United'.

Arsenal reached number 16 with 'Good Old Arsenal' in 1971, the year they beat Liverpool 2-1 in the FA Cup Final.

Nottingham Forest reached 24 in 1978 with 'We've Got The Whole World In Our Hands' the same year they beat Liverpool in the League Cup Final replay 1-0.

In 1975, West Ham beat Fulham 2-0 in the FA Cup Final, and scored a hit with a modern version of their 'I'm Forever Blowing Bubbles' theme song.

Everton have charted twice. With 'Here We Go' in 1985 when they lost to Manchester United in the FA Cup Final, and again in 1986, when they lost in the FA Cup Final again, this time to Liverpool (who also charted with their single).

Tottenham Hotspur have gained entry to the top 20 twice: with 'Ossie's Dream (Spurs Are On Their Way To Wembley)' in 1981; and with 'Tottenham Tottenham' in 1982.

Both times they won the FA Cup — first against Manchester City, then against Queens Park Rangers.

Manchester United and Liverpool have each charted three times.

In United's case, it was with 'Manchester United' in 1976, 'Glory Glory Man. United' in 1983. and 'We All Follow Man. United' in 1985. They lost the FA Cup 1-0 against Southampton, but won 4-0 against Brighton and 1-0 against Everton.

Liverpool's successes came in 1977 with their 'We Can Do It' EP, which included 'You'll Never Walk Alone'; in 1983 with 'Liverpool (We're Never Gonna . . .)'; and in 1986 with 'Sitting On Top Of The World'. They lost 2-0 in the FA Cup Final to United in 1977; got their own back in 1983 by beating them 2-1 in the Milk Cup; and beat Everton 3-1 in 1986, in the FA Cup.

Kevin Keegan had a hit with 'Head Over Heels In Love' in 1979 and Glenn Hoddle and Chris Waddle reached number 12 with 'Diamond Lights' in 1987.

England hit the charts with their "All the Way" record last year.

DENNIS WISE
WIMBLEDON

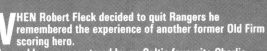

WHEN Robert Fleck decided to quit Rangers he remembered the experience of another former Old Firm scoring hero.

The problems encountered by ex-Celtic favourite Charlie Nicholas during his stormy spell at Arsenal convinced the stocky striker he should avoid the bright lights of London.

Instead he opted for the comparative peace and tranquillity of Norwich, undeterred by their rock bottom slot in the First Division.

FLECK FURY

'I've proved Rangers wrong'

That was bad news for Chelsea and Watford, who were both hot on his trail, but Fleck's arrival at Carrow Road was a significant factor in The Canaries' dramatic climb away from the relegation zone.

There's a world of difference between Norwich and Glasgow, where Fleck was born, raised and became a scoring sensation as a member of the Rangers side that clinched their first League title in nine years when Graeme Souness took charge.

But he maintains: "I have absolutely no regrets. I knew what I was doing when I decided to leave Ibrox and move to Norwich.

"I could have stayed at Rangers. They offered me a new contract, with very good money, but I just felt it was time for a change."

It's no secret that Fleck, a Scottish Under-21 cap, didn't always see eye to eye with Souness, although neither would dispute they were good for each other during that memorable Championship winning campaign.

Fleck contributed 19 goals towards the long-awaited League crown and showed he hadn't lost his scoring touch following his £580,000 move South of the border.

Not even a series of nagging injury problems could prevent him getting among the goals as Norwich did enough to preserve their First Division status.

The bold move by manager Dave Stringer, who inherited the reins after The Canaries' disastrous start cost Ken Brown his job, paid handsome dividends.

Fleck laughs: "I think I've proved a point or two to a few people. When Jock Wallace was manager at Ibrox he tried to sell me to Dundee for £25,000 but I turned it down. I always knew I could do better for myself.

"Norwich suits me fine. It may be a lot quieter than Glasgow, but they're an ambitious club with plenty of good players.

"I was delighted to repay their faith in me by scoring a few important goals to help them stay up. Now I'd like to think we can go on to win one of the big trophies this season."

WHAT an 'orrible lot you SHOOT readers are. Once upon a time we launched a new feature in the weekly magazine in which we invited your nominations for footballing lookalikes. We've since been inundated with postbag after postbag filled with wicked nominations.

The feature kicked off in February 1988 with Thomas McIntyre of Belfast pointing out that Ian Rush is a dead ringer for that well-known bringer of glad tidings Postman Pat. Subsequent gems paired together Paul Gascoigne with Dennis the Menace, Ruud Gullit with a Hungarian Puli dog, Robert Maxwell with Paddington Bear and Vinny Jones with that mild-mannered songstress Grace Jones.

Your most popular nominations have been Norman Whiteside's resemblance to Russ Abbot, Ian Rush (again) and John Aldridge's likeness to Paul Young lagging behind in third place. BORING!

Here's your latest, more original bunch and, as ever, we're sending fabulous SHOOT T-shirts to their nominees.

McMINDER

Anyone for Dennis? Dennis Waterman, actually, of Minder fame who, according to Dorothy Keogh of Roehampton . . . "is a dead ringer for balding England midfielder Steve McMahon."

JACK GETS A PLUG

Here's one to send Jack Charlton reaching for his famous black book, to enter the name of reader Alan Eltringham of Brough, North Humberside. Alan tells us: "My mum thinks Jack looks like Plug, one of the Bash Street Kids."

STAN CLAN

Still on Merseyside, here's another fine mess you've landed us in. Philip Rooney points out: "Steve Nicol is a reincarnation of Stan Laurel."

MARSH WALLOW

If you don't think that one is a hit, try this nomination from Daniel Booth, from Macclesfield: "Former Boxing World champion Terry Marsh has a striking resemblance to England defender Terry Butcher."

JIMMY RIDDLE

We can't take much more of this. Will Mark Cummins, from Dublin, bring us back to reality? "Have you noticed the resemblance between Bruce Forsyth and Jimmy Hill?"

MARTONY

Blow me — they get worse. Over to Todger (*Todger?*) Watkins, from Reading, who says: "Is Martina Navratilova really Tony Adams in disguise?"

WHO'S THE BOSS?

Thought not. Last chance goes to Mike Irwin from Harrow: "Your editor Peter Stewart looks like Blackburn manager Don Mackay."

GERRY'S TARGET
The first for Rovers

FORMER England captain Gerry Francis, made football history when he took over as player-manager at Bristol Rovers and also put up some of his own money to buy into the club as an associate director.

Born in Hammersmith, London, Gerry Francis played his first League game at the age of 16, in 1968, for Queens Park Rangers against Liverpool. By the age of 23 he was skipper of his country.

In 1976, he suffered a major back injury that kept him out of the game for two years.

In those days, osteopaths were viewed with suspicion, but Terry Moule, now a famous practitioner who has treated Sebastian Coe and Fatima Whitbread, saved Gerry's career.

Gerry, who could barely walk at the time, went to Moule as a last resort while waiting for an operation on his back.

The surgeon who was going to perform the operation was on holiday and Francis decided to try Terry Moule, who told him he'd have him playing again in three weeks' time.

Unbelievably, he did, and after two years in the wilderness, Gerry Francis was cured.

In 1979, after a year proving his fitness, he moved from QPR to Crystal Palace and Terry Venables for a fee of £500,000.

When Venables took over as manager of QPR, Gerry went with him, until in 1982 he was transferred to Coventry.

Later spells as player-coach at Crystal Palace, Coventry, QPR and Exeter, proved Francis's durability in the tough world of football.

After periods with Portsmouth, Swansea and Cardiff, Gerry took over as first team coach at Wimbledon. Then in July 1987 to Bristol Rovers as their new manager.

But what made Francis decide to join a club that regarded Third Division survival as an achievement?

"I enjoyed the times I played for Rovers. There's a great spirit here and it suited me," says Gerry.

"Bristol is a very big city, with its own TV and radio stations. It's a big media attraction, the people of Bristol like their football and I believe the club has potential.

"That's one of the reasons I decided to put £12,000 of my own money into the club.

"Maybe it's not the most sensible

ANDY REECE

thing to do, but it showed my faith in the club and helped to buy better players."

He brought Ian Holloway back from Wimbledon and signed on youngsters like goalkeeper Nigel Martyn, Andy Reece and Devon White, who was working as an electrician when Francis picked him up.

Despite his Rovers connection, Francis lives in Surrey with his girlfriend Lindsay.

"We do have a flat near Bath, but I don't intend moving to the area on a permanent basis as it's only about an hour's drive, along the M4, from where I live."

Gerry's other business interests include antiques, property development, and a football promotional company.

He also enjoys tennis, squash and retains an interest in racing pigeons, a legacy from his family life as a youngster in West London.

The highlight of his own playing career, was: "Being made captain of England at 23, and never having lost an international at Wembley."

Now Gerry hopes that sometime in the not too distant future his best achievement as a manager would be to take Bristol Rovers into the First Division.

EVERGREEN striker Frank Worthington has seen it all during a 21-year playing career spanning three decades.

It was towards the end of the 1960's that his rare talent was unearthed at Huddersfield; throughout the 1970's that he was at his goalscoring best; and during the 1980's that he has played for no fewer than eight League clubs.

And, even though he is coming up to his 40th birthday in November, there's every chance Worthy will go on playing into the 1990's.

"I love the game as much as I ever have done and still get the same kick from playing as I did 20 years ago.

"I'll call it a day if I ever become an embarrassment to myself, but at the moment I still have something to offer."

As long as he remains in the game Frank insists that he will continue to entertain saying: "People pay hard-earned money to watch football and they like to see something a little bit different.

"There aren't enough players entertaining themselves, but I intend to keep on doing so for as long as I can."

Believe it or not . . .

★ At the age of 39 Frank is the third oldest player in the League — behind Billy Bonds and Tommy Hutchison — and is currently playing for his ELEVENTH English club (Stockport).

★ Frank is the only player in the League today who has scored in each of the last 21 seasons — 1967–68 to 1987–88 inclusive.

★ He has now joined the elite band of professionals who have amassed over 750 League appearances. Frank passed his target towards the end of last season.

★ Worthy is now fast-approaching another milestone — that of 250

I WON'T QUIT!

Declares Frank Worthington

League goals. He is currently just 12 goals short of the impressive total.

★ Together with Stockport boss Asa Hartford the two have made in excess of 1,600 competitive apearances over the last 22 years.

FRANK'S FACTFILE		
Born: Halifax 23.11.48		
England: 8 caps; 2 goals		
Season	Club	Lge games/goals
1966–67	Huddersfield	3 —
1967–68	,,	29 5
1968–69	,,	16 4
1969–70	,,	42 19
1970–71	,,	42 9
1971–72	,,	39 5
1972–73	Leicester	39 10
1973–74	,,	42 20
1974–75	,,	42 18
1975–76	,,	39 9
1976–77	,,	41 14
1977–78	,,	7 1
1977–78	Bolton	35 11
1978–79	,,	42 24
1979–80	,,	7 —
1979–80	Birmingham	19 5
1980–81	,,	36 16
1981–82	,,	20 9
1981–82	Leeds	17 9
1982–83	,,	15 5
1982–83	Sunderland	19 2
1983–84	Southampton	34 4
1984–85	Brighton	31 7
1985–86	Tranmere	42 18
1986–87	,,	17 3
1986–87	Preston	11 3
1987–88	,,	12 —
1987–88	Stockport	6
Total		238

A fascinating comparison of the skills and strengths of Brian Clough and his talented son Nigel.

SHOOTING

Brian preferred close-range shooting to taking pot shots from outside the box. He was lethal once inside the penalty area and the fact that he rattled in 251 goals in just 274 League matches for Middlesbrough and Sunderland is a measure of his stunning accuracy.
Rating: 9 out of 10.
Nigel does not possess blistering power in his shots but he makes up for that with his placement and accuracy. He uses the minimum possible backlift so he is capable of whipping the ball towards goal very swiftly.
Rating: 7 out of 10.

HEADING

He stood 5ft. 11in. and weighed 11st. 12lbs. at his peak, which is two inches taller and half a stone heavier than Nigel. But Brian was never a really dominant player in the air. Although capable of launching powerful air raids when necessary, he preferred the ball to be played to his feet.
Rating: 7 out of 10.
His lack of inches is an obvious disadvantage, yet he manages to hold his own in the air. He is not an exceptionally powerful header of the ball but is always ready to challenge for the high crosses.
Rating: 7 out of 10.

SPEED

Brian used to lure defenders into a false sense of security with an almost lazy stride when first settling on the ball, but then he would suddenly put his foot down on the accelerator and for a short but vital distance become as fast as any player in the game.
Rating: 8 out of 10.
Nigel possesses great speed off the mark and can lose close markers with a devastating burst of pace. Especially quick on the turn. He is always willing to chase the hopeful long ball and make decoy runs to draw opponents.
Rating: 8 out of 10.

PASSING

Brian rarely wanted to give the ball away once he had got possession so passing was not one of his strongest points, but he perfected the wall pass technique – and behold any player who did not return the ball to him once he had made his run into space! He could hit accurate long passes but only when he had to.
Rating: 7 out of 10.
Nigel is an unselfish player who sets up many chances for colleagues with fine control and precision passing. Has superb vision with the ability to hit long and short accurate passes. And with players like Franz Carr and Neil Webb around that can have a devastating effect on the opposition.
Rating: 8 out of 10.

POSITIONING

He was one of the old-style centre-forwards who would rove to shake off his centre-half. Colleagues always found it easy to hit him with passes because he was such an intelligent positional

player and an ideal target man. Brian would make sure that if there was any space to be found he would sniff it out.
Rating: 8 out of 10.
Nigel's positional sense is improving all the time and he is always looking for space in which to operate. He has some of his father's goalscorer's instinct, and is never far away when a ball rebounds. His lack of experience is still sometimes exposed by some of the wiser First Division defenders.
Rating: 7 out of 10.

FLAIR

Brian's flair lay in his gift for scoring goals. There were no frills and unnecessary skills in his game. All he was interested in was taking the quickest route to goal and you never saw him wasting time with intricate play. As brave and as strong as a lion, his motto was: "Let's get on with it."

Rating: 7 out of 10.
Nigel is a no-nonsense player who gets on with the game with the minimum amount of fuss. Living and playing under a strict disciplinarian like Brian must have squashed any shows of arrogance and flashy behaviour very early in his career. He has developed into a model professional – a credit to his Dad.
Rating: 7 out of 10.

TEMPERAMENT

He was a born competitor who would run through brick walls for the glory of a goal. There were flashes of quick temper from him but he used to take it out on the opposition by trying that much harder to beat them. He was a headstrong person because he relied on his big ego to help motivate him. Nothing has changed!
Rating: 8 out of 10.
It is still early in his career to assess Nigel in this department, but he does seem to have a cool, mature head on his young shoulders. Like so many youngsters, he can let his head drop when the pressure's on but he is finding it easier to cope as he grows in confidence and he never gives less than 100 per cent.
Rating: 8 out of 10.

Proud father Brian with striker son Nigel.

H AND SON

NIGEL

Has superb vision

GOAL POACHING

Brian was one of the hungriest players in the game. He seemed to grow a foot taller in the penalty box and was prepared to knock anybody – including team-mates – out of the way to get a shot in at goal. His scoring rate was just phenomenal. Goals were food and drink to him and he enjoyed many a banquet.
Rating: 10 out of 10.
He is not, as yet, a prolific goalscorer but topping the 20 mark last season is proof of his sharpness in and around the six yard box. He is brave and is always willing to challenge for any ball, but his lack of physical strength often means that he misses out on vital chances. He doesn't rate with his Dad – but who does?
Rating: 8 out of 10.

SKILL

He didn't often dwell on the ball, but he had the ability to go past defenders and was particularly skilful at bringing it under control when it was played up to him regardless of the attention of close-marking defenders.
Rating: 8 out of 10.
Nigel is blessed with fine close control and he shields the ball very well. This means he is difficult to dispossess and he can buy time for his team-mates to find open spaces. He is a very tidy player and possesses good basic skills.
Rating: 8 out of 10.

SUMMARY

Our ratings show a 72–68 verdict in favour of Brian Clough. Brian was unlucky that he did not have the First Division stage to play on more often. Most of his goals were scored in the Second Division and he was top Second Division scorer three years in succession. Capped twice by England, a knee injury brought a premature end to his career and it is football's good fortune that he took the direct, confident approach that marked his play into management. Nigel has a fine career stretching ahead of him and has the sort of attitude and determination that suggest he is going to get better and may one day become as effective a force as Cloughie Senior used to be. Like father, like son.

Fash the Cash

HE'S been called Fash the Bash, much to his displeasure. Well, how about this one: Fash the Cash!

John Fashanu has one of football's most heartwarming rags to riches stories thanks to a determination that is the epitome of his side Wimbledon's own rise from the Southern League to last season's FA Cup Final winners.

Fash now lives in a £600,000 mansion in Hampstead – one of London's most exclusive areas – and runs his own import/export business.

But it hasn't always been the good life for the explosive 26-year-old striker.

Born in London, Fashanu spent his kindergarten years in a Dr Barnardo children's home.

Then, aged five, he left the capital to be brought up by foster parents in the rural backwaters of Norfolk.

It was with local club Norwich that Fashanu's footballing career began, along with his brother Justin.

But while Justin was transferred to Nottingham Forest in a £1 million move, John's career was still some way from earning him a superstar lifestyle.

He made only seven League appearances for The Canaries in over four seasons and, after a loan spell with Crystal Palace, joined Lincoln City for a small fee.

"Sometimes you have to take one step back in order to take two steps forwards," he explains.

"It made sense to leave Norwich at the time. I had to stop being Justin's kid brother and find my own identity."

He scored 11 goals in 36 League games for Lincoln, and returned to London to join Millwall in 1984.

It was at The Den, under the guidance of manager George Graham, that Fashanu's career began taking shape. To such an extent that Wimbledon parted with a then-record transfer fee of £175,000 to land him in 1986.

Now, after helping The Dons complete their rise into the First Division and, even better, an FA Cup Final victory against Liverpool, he's being described as a £1 million pound player and a possible England international alternative to Mark Hateley. His own personal fortune can't be far behind the magic seven figure total by now.

He's easily Wimbledon's highest paid player with a contract reputed to be worth £2,000 a week.

And then there's his off-the-field activities, where his articulate, charming and witty character make him an attractive commercial proposition.

You'll see his face in newspapers and magazines, and regularly on television talk shows and quiz shows.

His temperament is ideally suited to the big-time.

"But please don't call me Fash the Flash. The simple fact is that I'm not the type to be affected by nerves. I never have been."

Fash the Cash? That'll do nicely . . . not that he doesn't work for it.

Fashanu's charm off the pitch makes him an easily marketable asset.

His dedication to personal fitness for football is well-known. He keeps his 6 feet 1 inch frame fighting fit with regular work-outs at a gym. He's even sparred in a boxing ring with Lloyd Honeyghan and Errol Christie.

He doesn't drink, doesn't smoke, and pays close attention to his diet.

"And after training with the Wimbledon squad I often stay behind to work on my finishing," he adds.

After all that Fashanu somehow finds time to concentrate on his business ventures.

It sometimes involves staying up until 2.30 on a Saturday morning . . . just over 12 hours before First Division matches.

He explains: "I use Friday evenings to catch up on my paperwork. I've an office at home, I take the 'phones (yes, he's got more than one 'phone) off the hook and I get down to some pretty hard work at my desk.

"I find the best time to work is at the still of the night when there are no distractions. And there is something very satisfying about seeing a huge pile of papers gradually whittled away to nothing.

"Sometimes it's 2.30 in the morning before I finish and get to bed. But lack of sleep has never been a problem. I'm still able to give 110 per cent in every game I play."

Few would disagree with that.

FASH THE BASH:
Southampton's Derek Statham feels the full weight of a Fashanu challenge.

TONY CASCARINO

Millwall

MISER McLEAN'S BEST BUY

S COTTISH football's cash registers have never been busier with millions of pounds changing hands in a thriving market.

But while Old Firm giants Rangers and Celtic can comfortably afford to splash out king-size sums on new talent, clubs like Dundee United are forced to be more prudent with their spending.

Tannadice boss Jim McLean, out on his own as the Premier Division's longest-serving manager, could never be accused of extravagance in 17 years at the helm.

He has worked wonders on a shoestring budget as United have regularly competed on equal terms with the giants of Europe, claiming some famous scalps along the way.

One of McLean's best deals was a triumph for persistence as much for his ability to spot star potential and there has rarely been a bigger bargain than midfield star Hamish French.

Twice he rejected moves to Tayside, preferring instead to remain with Highland League club Keith while also pursuing a career as a British Telecom engineer.

But McLean refused to take no for an answer and in the summer of 1987 he gladly forked out £20,000 to make it third time lucky as French succumbed to the temptation of top flight football.

Debut

The new boy made a sensational debut with a starring display as United gained a hard fought point thanks to a 1-1 draw with Rangers, the reigning Champions, at Ibrox.

But within 48 hours disaster struck. French broke a leg in a freak training incident and was sidelined for 16 games.

"You could say I learned the hard way," he says, "but it was really down to the fact that my reactions weren't sharp enough for the Premier Division.

"It was all very frustrating, especially as I was a late starter and keen to make an impact.

"I don't regret turning United down the first or second time they wanted me. I was keen to prove myself in the Highland League and then I wanted to qualify as a BT engineer.

"I didn't want to turn the boss down when he came in for me the third time. Besides, I was a fully qualified telephone engineer by then and I knew I had something to fall back on if things didn't work out at Tannadice."

Thankfully for all concerned, French is on the right lines.

Hamish French has proved to be a bargain buy for Dundee United manager Jim McLean.

A DAY IN TH
TERRY

BEING captain of Rangers has got to be the most demanding job in soccer. I now know that you could make a full-time living out of it without ever kicking a football.

I'm not sure exactly how many supporters clubs we have world wide, but I do know that it runs into three figures. And that's an awful lot of fans to keep happy.

It was a tremendous honour when Graeme Souness asked me to be his skipper immediately after signing me from Ipswich two years ago.

But although I had been captain at Portman Road, nothing could have prepared me for what I had let myself in for.

I was simply overwhelmed with invitations, fan mail and autograph requests from all four corners of the globe.

In my first few weeks in Glasgow I shook more hands than the Prime Minister at election time. I developed writers' cramp from signing my name so many times.

I didn't want anyone to get the impression that I was some kind of precious English superstar who didn't have time for the fans. So I personally replied to every letter I received and accepted all the invitations.

But I soon realised it was an impossible task. I could spend my life opening supermarkets and presenting trophies at supporters club functions, but it wouldn't leave any time for training or playing.

So now I have a secretary to help with my mail. And although I still attend two or three functions a week, I try to keep some time free for my family.

E LIFE OF
BUTCHER

Thankfully the fans appreciate the situation. They know I'm doing my best and realise I would never snub a genuine fan.

That's why my wife, Rita, hates it when we go shopping together. She wheels the trolley and buys all the food while I sign autographs for the housewives.

My sons, Christopher and Edward, loved it when I broke a leg just over a year ago. It meant I was at home all day to play with them.

But Rita was as delighted as me when I finally received the all clear to resume training because after months of enforced inactivity I was like a bear with a sore head.

It was around that time that rumours started circulating that I was unhappy at Rangers and wanted to go back to an English club.

Nothing could have been further from the truth and I finally nailed those lies when I signed an extension to my contract which will effectively keep me at Ibrox for the rest of my playing career.

I love it here in Scotland and so do all my family. A lot of people down south cannot understand how an England international can leave the Football League, but the standard of football up here is just as high and the quality of life

Continued overleaf

is tremendous.

We live in a beautiful house in the heart of the Stirlingshire countryside, yet we're only 30 miles from Glasgow so it doesn't take more than half an hour to drive to the ground.

My England team-mate Chris Woods lives nearby, so we often travel in together for training, which takes place no more than goal kick away from Ibrox Stadium.

We train for two or three hours most mornings under the supervision of assistant manager Walter Smith and coach Doug Livermore.

And the fact that Graeme Souness is the gaffer doesn't earn him any special favours on the training ground.

He has to work as hard as the rest of us and probably gets more stick than anyone if he gets something wrong, particularly from Ray Wilkins.

A lot of people have the wrong impression of Graeme. There's no denying that he puts himself about on the pitch, but he's not the hard case he's made out to be.

When you get to know him you soon realise that he is a genuine bloke with a wicked sense of humour.

If Graeme is playing, the running of the team is left to Walter Smith, who learned his trade under Jim Mclean at Dundee United.

He's the man who'll call the shots during the half-time interval. He's also in charge of the substitutions, although I must confess I can't remember a time when he's hauled the Boss off!

After the game, I'm usually expected to go the sponsors lounge to have a chat with some of the people who have put their money into the club.

Public relations is a very important part of my job as Rangers captain and it's important I make the right impression on and off the field.

I got into a lot of trouble when I was sent-off against Celtic in that infamous match, but everyone connected with the club stood by me magnificently.

Chairman David Holmes even asked if I wanted to leave when I was charged with conduct likely to cause a breach of the peace after that game.

He didn't want me to leave, but was so concerned about my welfare that he was prepared to let me go if I was unhappy.

That offer made me realise just what a special club I had joined when I signed for Rangers.

So much has happened in my two years at Ibrox and not all of it has been good. But I wouldn't change a thing and I want to make this club the most feared in Europe.

SOUNESS SHOCKED ME

confesses John Brown

JOHN BROWN thought he was hearing things when he picked up the phone and found Graeme Souness on the end of the line.

"I thought he must have got the wrong number," laughs the £350,000 Ibrox midfielder, "It never crossed my mind that Rangers would want to sign me."

Brown was still in a state of shock as he travelled to Glasgow to complete the transfer formalities. And he admits: "It was only after my debut at Hearts that it sunk in. I really was a Rangers player!"

Brown's burning ambition to taste soccer success prompted him to seek a move from Dundee, for whom he was a constant driving force. "I badly wanted to get among the honours," he points out.

"No disrespect to Dundee, they're a smashing little outfit, but I'd reached the point in my career when I had to think about myself.

"I want to be a winner and the opportunity to join Rangers, the team I supported as a youngster, was simply too good to miss. It's the perfect move for me."

The strong-tackling, 26-year-old could be a key figure in the Ibrox giants' bid to

Graeme Souness

regain their League crown.

In three and a half years at Dens Park he averaged almost one goal in every three games – including, whisper it, a hat-trick against Rangers!

At previous club Hamilton Accies he won a place in Scottish football's record books when, at the age of 18, he netted the only other hat-trick of his career – against Berwick Rangers – when operating as a full-back!

So Brown certainly knows the way to goal and explains: "Graeme Souness is looking to me to score a few for Rangers. At the moment Ally McCoist is shouldering the bulk of the responsibility and I'd like to weigh in with my share.

"The boss wants me to get into the opposition penalty box whenever possible. He wants to see me getting shots and headers on target and I'm confident in my ability to score goals."

In 1986–87 Brown almost joined Hearts but the transfer collapsed at the eleventh hour when the Edinburgh club were dissatisfied with x-rays of the player's knees.

"That was a shattering experience," he recalls. "I'd had one or two operations earlier in my career and never gave them a second thought. When I was told the news it was the worst thing that had ever happened to me."

But Brown quickly put the blow behind him to roar back to form with rejuvenated Dundee, although the nightmare returned to haunt him again when Rangers moved in for his signature.

"I had a few sleepless nights worrying if there would be a problem," he adds. "I was also off my food and it was a tremendous relief when they said I'd passed the medical.

"Now my main priority is to hold down a regular place at Ibrox. I badly want to show that I'm good enough to play at this level and justify the faith Rangers have shown in me."

Razor Sharp

ASK any Everton player what he thinks of Graeme Sharp and the reply will be unanimous: "He's the best centre-forward in Britain."

In fact the Scottish striker's reputation stretches further than Merseyside these days with football followers nationwide singing the praises of the Glaswegian goal-grabber.

But it's been a bumpy ride to the top for Sharpshooter Graeme who has had a constant battle to make the Everton number nine shirt his own.

From Latchford to Lineker, though, he has seen them all off during an eight-year career at Goodison which has had more ups and downs than a ride on the big dipper.

Injuries have also threatened his supremacy and during Everton's last Championship-winning season, 1986/87, he was restricted to just 28 League appearances – and a meagre five goals.

But he was back to his bustling best last term, hitting more than 20 League and Cup goals despite playing in a side struggling to find the consistency they had displayed the previous year.

"There are strikers who get more goals than Graeme but for all-round ability he's the tops," says team-mate and midfield provider Kevin Sheedy.

"I have always rated Graeme very highly, considering him to be the best centre-forward in the First Division, and he confirmed my opinion of him last season.

"You often find that teams with out and out goalscorers don't win anything and that it's sides with strikers of all-round ability who are the most successful.

"And although Everton ended up with nothing last term it was through no fault of Graeme. In fact he was probably our most consistent player and one of the few who emerged from a disappointing season with any great credit.

"The reason we didn't win anything was because the midfield players didn't get their share of the goals."

Triumphs

In Everton's two Championship triumphs of the 80s the goals which brought the glory days back to Goodison came from all departments. When they won the title in 1987 Kevin, together with Trevor Steven and Adrian Heath all weighed in with vital goals.

"That didn't happen last season and we must all take a share of the blame," says Eire international Sheedy. "Graeme did his bit but didn't get the support he deserved.

"That's why I disagree with the view that we need a new striker to become Championship material again.

"We have the side to be successful once more provided the midfield players do their job and get the goals which would relieve the pressure on the lads up front."

At 6ft. 1in. tall the Scottish international is always going to

Ian Rush could have been an Everton star.

pose an aerial threat to any defence, but it's not just for his heading ability that Sharp is feared.

"He also has terrific control and holds the ball up well until support is available," adds Sheedy. "We wouldn't swap him for anyone."

That view would doubtless be backed up by former Everton boss Gordon Lee, the man responsible for bringing Sharp to Goodison Park in 1980.

Lee has gone on record as saying that his bargain buy is now the most complete centre-forward in Europe. "At the time I bought him I had to decide between Graeme and Ian Rush," he recalls. "And despite what has happened since I still think I made the right decision."

Whether you agree with the former Goodison chief or not there's no denying that Sharp has repaid the £150,000 Everton invested several times over.

Kevin Sheedy accepts some of the blame for Everton's lack of success last season.

Maine R

Manchester City sl
course for the First

Yo-yo club Manchester City are hoping promotion back to the First Division will prove to be kids stuff.

The Maine Road youngsters who scooped the FA Youth Cup in 1986 by defeating fiercest rivals Manchester United found themselves thrown in at the deep end.

City, millions of pounds in debt after a series of disastrous excursions into the transfer market, had no alternative but to blood the kids before they were ready.

A year after their champagne success in the country's premier youth competition, therefore, City's talented teenagers were brought crashing back to earth as the club took the plunge into the Second Division.

With new manager Mel Machin at the helm City just failed to last the course in

Mel Machin

the 1987–88 promotion campaign. But the attitude at Maine Road is that it's only a matter of time before the club are back in the big time.

Machin rejected the security of a new contract at Norwich City, where he was Ken Brown's right hand man, to take on the challenge of restoring the club's former glories.

One of the main reasons behind his drop into the Second Division was the vast array of talent on City's books. "It wasn't a difficult decision," he admitted.

Further proof of City's rich potential was their reserves' triumph in the Central League, finishing ahead of First Division giants like Liverpool, Everton and neighbours United to clinch the 1987 title.

Now there's a feeling of great

City starlet in defence—the talented Steve Redmond.

oad ahead!

kers are on
Division

Ian Brightwell and David White (below left) have both pledged their support to City.

optimism that the City slickers have matured to the point where they can tackle the man-sized job of steering the club back to the top level.

The biggest problem, however, is ensuring that none of the promising talent is transferred elsewhere. Liverpool manager Kenny Dalglish heads a long list of top bosses waiting to pounce at the slightest sign of encouragement from the Maine Road hierarchy.

But City chairman Peter Swales promises: "We reluctantly sold Paul Stewart last June, but we are determined to keep all our best players. The current crop of youngsters is the best we've ever had at this club and they're not for sale.

"Our future is wrapped up in these lads. We would only be cutting our throats in the long term if we cashed in on any of them."

Swales rubber-stamped the type of deals in the past that put City firmly on top of the hard-up league. At one point their debt rose to a staggering £4 million after lavish spending sprees by former bosses Malcolm Allison and John Bond.

"Our financial situation is still not the best in the business but it is improving," Swales reports. "The last working year saw us make a profit of £600,000 and we'll keep plugging away until we're back in the black again."

One of the most sought-after Maine Road youngsters is left-back Andy Hinchcliffe but he put a prompt end to transfer rumours by committing himself to a long-term contract.

Paul Lake, Ian Brightwell, David White, Steve Redmond, Paul Moulden and Ian Scott are others who have pledged their futures to City.

Hinchcliffe, White and Redmond underlined their potential last season when they were successive winners of the Barclays Young Eagle awards.

City might have missed out on promotion last term but their 10–1 thrashing of bottom club Huddersfield earned them a place in football's record books.

White and co-strikers Paul Stewart and Tony Adcock, who later switched to Northampton in an exchange deal with Trevor Morley, all notched hat-tricks as City went goal crazy.

What a pity Machin's men couldn't sustain the form they showed in a whirlwind six-week period that saw them hammer 36 goals in 11 games to shoot into the promotion reckoning.

But not even a subsequent form slump that put paid to their promotion prospects could stop City dreaming of a return, sooner rather than later, to the First Division.

"There isn't a more ambitious club in the country," Machin adds. "We know what we want and we have the players to enable us to achieve it.

"The youngsters did a lot of growing up last season and learned many valuable lessons. I've a feeling their education is almost complete."

DINHA

BRILLIANT Brazilian Mirandinha may not have made the dramatic impact on the English First Division that Newcastle fans were hoping for, but the player himself believes he's done enough to persuade more of his fellow-countrymen to bring their talents to Britain.

Of course he's had his problems on Tyneside where the goals have failed to flow in the way they once threatened early in the season — but by no stretch of the imagination can Dinha be considered an expensive flop.

Newcastle fans have taken him to their hearts and he's as much a local hero as Paul Gascoigne or Neil McDonald. There's even a hint of Geordie in his Brazilian accent.

Having completed his first season at St. James' Park the samba sensation has time to reflect on his decision to become the first player from Brazil to try his luck in England. And he clearly has no regrets.

"I have settled here very well and have had no cause to regret coming to this country," he says. "Of course I would like to have been more successful last season but I am happy with the way I have adapted to what has been a whole new way of life. Everyone seems to think I would have problems but I would like to think I have proved to other players in Brazil that England is a good place to play football.

"I think I have been a good ambassador for my country and that other Brazilians will follow my lead. I would certainly have no hesitation in inviting some of them to join me over here."

In the past it has been Latin countries such as Spain, Italy and even Portugal which have benefited from the import of Brazilian talent — while England has had to settle for its coffee.

But thanks to Mirandinha, and the men who helped set up ambitious transfer from Palmeiras to Newcastle, that could all be about to change.

Towards the end of last season Dundee United made a dramatic bid to land World Cup full-back Josimar and, for a time, were convinced they'd secured the big man's signature. But at the death the player opted for the Spanish sunshine in Seville.

The tragic turn-around of events left the Scottish club bitter and bewildered but, according to Mirandinha, there are more Brazilians prepared to pack their bags and come to Britain.

MITE

"I know of a number of players who are considering the idea – Nelsinho and Carlos to name but two – and providing clubs over here are prepared to take the risk then there could be quite an influx of Brazilian talent.

"I can see the trend switching from Italy, or Spain to England because I have shown that things such as the climate and the playing conditions can be overcome."

Playing in a Newcastle side which struggled for most of the season and was desperately short of confidence, Mirandinha was not as effective as he might have been in a team chasing the major honours.

But his neat control, arrogance, speed and shooting power were enough to convince manager Willie McFaul that the £500,000 he splashed out was a shrewd investment.

Newcastle fans can only hope that the club can hang on to the likes of Mirandinha, Gascoigne and McDonald and then use more of the £1.9 million received from Liverpool for Peter Beardsley to create a team worthy of such talent. No club deserves success more than Newcastle and their long suffering supporters.

In these days of freedom of contract, agents, multiple managerial changes and European poachers, many players clock up more clubs than Sevvy Ballesteros.

Even if a player isn't moved on by a new boss who wants to bring in his favourite right-back, the temptations to ask for a transfer are obvious.

So it is refreshing that not all players feel the need to constantly change to fresh pastures and the promise of greater riches, when their club falls on hard times.

Kevin Ratcliffe
(Everton)

KEVIN Ratcliffe has experienced both the highs and lows of professional football during his career with Everton.

At 24-years-old he found himself captain of an Everton side that was struggling near the bottom of the table, attracting four-figure gates and desperately low in morale.

But just four months later he led that team to FA Cup Final success over Watford in May 1984 to begin the Blue revival that has seen him lift a series of trophies.

Ratcliffe is also skipper of Wales having been first capped after he had played only a handful of games for Everton, who he joined as an apprentice.

The longest-serving member of the Goodison squad, he celebrated with a testimonial in 1988.

David O'Leary
(Arsenal)

DAVID O'Leary has been the cornerstone of Arsenal's defence for the last 13 seasons, his career spanning the late seventies successes of Terry Neill to the current ones under manager George Graham.

O'Leary joined Arsenal as one of the trio of Irish youngsters (Liam Brady and Frank Stapleton were the others) that had such an effect on the Neill side.

But while Brady and Stapleton went elsewhere, both home and abroad, during the lean years at Highbury, O'Leary remained and was rewarded with Arsenal's Littlewoods Cup triumph over Liverpool in 1987.

London-born, but Dublin-bred, O'Leary, who has collected more than 40 caps for the Republic of Ireland, epitomises all that is good about the game.

Rarely will you see him lose his temper with either team-mate or opponent and his off-field behaviour is just as impeccable.

Alan Cork
(Wimbledon)

ALAN CORK is the sole survivor at Wimbledon from the team that began life in the Football League back in 1977–78.

The joke down in SW19 is that 'Corky's' rapidly receding hairstyle is the result of the worry induced by nearly 350 League games for The Dons on their path up, down, and up again through the divisions.

"Not true," he says. "I looked 50 when I was only 18." He was actually born in 1959 and arrived at Plough Lane 19 years later after a brief flirtation with hometown-club Derby County.

More than 150 goals later he celebrated his testimonial season with an FA Cup Final triumph against Champions Liverpool last season.

L FAMILY

Mel Sterland
(Sheffield Wednesday)

SHEFFIELD Wednesday captain Mel Sterland is the last surviving member at Hillsborough of the squad that gained promotion from Division Three under Jack Charlton in 1980 at the start of the club's revival.

A former apprentice, Sheffield-born Sterland had made his debut the previous season and has appeared in more than 300 matches since for the club.

The rampaging full-back was a member of the England Under-21 team which triumphed in the 1984 European Championships.

Had he moved on to a bigger club Sterland may well have made the full England breakthrough but he has stayed at Hillsborough and surely his loyalty to Wednesday will one day be rewarded with a major honour.

Ricky Hill
(Luton)

RICKY Hill was rewarded for his loyalty to Luton Town last season when he collected a Littlewoods Cup winner's medal at Wembley.

Hill has been with the Bedfordshire club since 1973, making more than 400 League appearances. His only honours in that time have been a Second Division Championship medal and three England caps.

Had the talented midfielder opted for a move to one of the country's glamour clubs there is little doubt that he, like team-mate Brian Stein, would have a larger set of caps in his wardrobe.

Instead Hill chose to remain at Kenilworth Road, where he has always been a fan's favourite and it was fitting that he recovered from a broken leg in time to help Luton to that Wembley success over Arsenal in April 1988.

GO

RDON'S A GEM

STAMFORD Bridge fans will see the best of Gordon Durie now that he has laid the ghost of former Chelsea favourite David Speedie.

That's the view of his skipper and fellow Scot Joe McLaughlin who believes that it has taken the former Hibs star two years to make his mark in the big city.

"In his first season at the club so much was expected of him because he'd earned a reputation in Scotland and we had paid £400,000 for him," says Joe. "But he never really set the heather on fire.

"Everyone needs time to settle in at a new club but Gordon struggled more than most because he didn't come to terms with the pace of the game down here.

"Suddenly the fans were asking what the fuss was about with this so-called world-beater we'd bought from Hibernian and a couple of injury setbacks added to his problems."

At the end of Durie's first season at the Bridge, his striking rival David Speedie made his inevitable departure to seemingly open the door for the Paisley-born striker.

But just as Chelsea struggled last season so did Durie.

"He was starting to show his true colours midway through the season when he got a bad injury," recalls his club captain. "The timing was even more unfortunate because he seemed to be forging a dangerous partnership with Kerry Dixon.

Stronger team

"We were not the same team without him and, of all the injured players we had, we missed Gordon most. When he came back towards the end of the season he started scoring goals again and we looked a stronger team.

"By the end of the season I feel he had finally shaken off the Speedie replacement tag and the fans started to rate him as a good player in his own right. I am a Gordon Durie fan and believe he is international class.

"He's a tremendous all-round player and I believe the club should make every effort to keep Gordon and Kerry Dixon together because as a partnership they have the potential to be even better than Dixon and Speedie.

"Gordon is very different to David and while he may lack the aggression of the Coventry striker he has more skill and is arguably a better finisher. Now he has adapted to the English style of football he will go from strength to strength."

Durie's own personal problems were obviously not helped by the behind-the-scenes traumas which made Chelsea FC a football laughing stock last season. The club's running battle with the national Press must have made Durie wonder whether he had made the right decision joining London's fallen giants.

With speculation about his future making back page news on a number of occasions towards the end of the season, Chelsea fans may have thought they were going to lose the man they had just taken to their hearts.

A host of top clubs were rumoured to be interested in the million-pound rated Scottish international but, according to McLaughlin, Durie's future still lies at Stamford Bridge.

"Gordon has got six years of his contract to run and if Chelsea are to be great again it is vital we hang on to him and players of his ability," say Joe.

"Kerry only has a year to run on his contract but it would obviously be in the club's best interests to keep the partnership together and enable it to flourish."

Durie began last season in fine form helping Chelsea to second place in the table with ten goals in the first 12 games. Then came the slump followed by a knee injury which kept him out of action for almost four months.

He returned to the side in time to lend a valuable hand to Chelsea's fight against relegation and confirm his elevation to Andy Roxburgh's Scotland squad. After a disappointing first two seasons at Stamford Bridge, the future looks a sight rosier for Gordon Durie.

Chelsea fans will be hoping that Durie's partnership with Kerry Dixon will take the club back to the top.

SOC
WORLD

It wasn't me ref. Napoli's Salvatore Bagini pleads innocence against Juventus in the millionaire football world of Italy.

ABOVE: Rain or shine – where England go the British media follow. But Bobby Robson and Jimmy Hill can count themselves a little unlucky to find a rain storm in Israel. BELOW: A team talk for one of the Kuwaiti League clubs but we are not sure Brian Clough would fancy the manager's training gear.

CER
WIDE

ABOVE: The African nations are now emerging as a force in the soccer world. Two of their most promising countries are Morocco and Cameroon. BELOW: The rattles may be absent from the English football scene now but in Nigeria they still like to rattle and roll.

PENALTY PLON

Infamous spot-kick misses

GEOFF HURST

(For West Ham United v Stoke, Football League Cup, Semi-Final, Second Leg. December 15, 1971)

THERE were three minutes of extra-time remaining, the aggregate scores were level at 2-2, when England goalkeeper Gordon Banks fumbled a cross and pulled Hammers winger Harry Redknapp down into the Upton Park mud.

Up stepped Geoff Hurst, scorer of a penalty in the first-leg, to take the spot-kick.

Banks went to his right, and fisted the shot over the bar for one of the greatest saves of of his career.

It took two more matches before Stoke won through to their first Wembley Final where they beat Chelsea 2-1. In the second replay yet another penalty was awarded. It was saved by Bobby Moore, standing-in for the injured Bobby Ferguson only for Mike Bernard to run in and score.

BARCELONA

(v Steaua Bucharest in European Cup Final, May 7, 1986)

IT HAD seemed, at least according to the whole of Spain, that Terry Venables' Barcelona had only to turn up in Seville's Pizjuan Stadium to collect the European Cup for the first time.

But with no score after 120 minutes of cautious play and petty fouls the game went to penalties.

In a bizarre shoot-out – Barcelona's first four efforts were astonishingly saved by 'keeper Ducadam, while Steaua converted their third and fourth to secure victory.

El Tel, whose side had defeated Gothenburg 5-4 in a penalty shoot-out to reach the Final ruefully reflected: ''Against Gothenburg the players couldn't wait to take the penalties but tonight they were very nervous.''

BRIAN McCLAIR

(for Manchester United v Arsenal in FA Cup Fifth Round, 20 February, 1988)

WHEN Brian McClair arrived at Manchester United at the start of last season, he insisted he would not set himself any targets.

However, there is one target, the goal in front of Arsenal's famous North Bank at Highbury, that haunts McClair.

Arsenal were leading 2-1 in the FA Cup fifth round tie when McClair (having already scored), blazed a last minute penalty over the bar, and with it United's last hopes of major trophy success last season.

Little compensation that McClair ended the season with 24 League goals. The first United player to top 20 since George Best in 1967–68.

CLIVE WALKER

(for Sunderland v Norwich in Milk Cup Final at Wembley, 24 March, 1985)

CLIVE WALKER made history for Sunderland in the 1985 Milk Cup Final – for the wrong reason. He became the first player to miss a penalty in a Wembley Final.

Asa Hartford had given Norwich the lead early in the second-half, but almost immediately Sunderland were given the penalty lifeline when Dennis Van Wyk handled Barry Venison's cross.

Walker, who had scored two spectacular goals in the Semi-Finals, grazed the outside of a post and was branded the villain as Norwich City went on to win the Cup by the single goal.

Brian McClair misses against Arsenal and Manchester United crash out of the 1987 FA Cup.

KERS

DON MASSON

(for Scotland v Peru in the World Cup, at Cordoba, Argentina, 3 June, 1978)

IN THE space of a few months Scotland's Don Masson turned from penalty hero to villain.

It was Masson who scored from the spot in the vital qualifying match against Wales which ensured Scotland's passage to the World Cup in Argentina.

However, with the scores level at 1-1 in their opening group games with Peru, Scotland were awarded a penalty. Masson took the kick but it was a feeble effort which goalkeeper Quiroga saved comfortably. Peru, now inspired, went on to win 3-1.

Masson was dropped and Scotland went out.

ZICO

(for Brazil v France, 1986 World Cup Quarter Final, Guadalajara, Mexico, June 21, 1988)

ZICO will be remembered as one of those players who could turn games with a flash of genius. But his own dream of winning a World Cup winner's medal was shattered just as quickly in the Quarter-Finals of his last tournament.

In the 70th minute of this pulsating clash, Zico, on the bench because of a niggling injury, came on with the scores level 1-1. With his first touch, he sent Branco into the penalty area to be brought down by French 'keeper Bats.

Zico himself took the penalty, but he put it tamely wide.

The match went on to penalties and, although Zico scored this time, team-mates Socrates and Cezar missed and the French won the shoot-out 4-3.

GRAHAM RIX

(for Arsenal v Valencia in European Cup Winners' Cup Final, Brussels, 14 May, 1980)

GRAHAM RIX'S penalty miss proved to be the killer blow in a season of marathon endeavour for Arsenal.

The battle weary Gunners, facing Valencia just four days after their shock FA Cup Final defeat by then Second Division West Ham United, were playing their 69th game of the season.

The Brussels Final remained deadlocked throughout barren periods of normal and extra-time and even after a penalty first round of five shots for each side.

With the competition into sudden death and the score standing 5-4 in Valencia's favour it was left for Rix to keep Arsenal's hopes alive.

His shot was parried by 'keeper Pereira and Arsenal were left empty-handed after a season that had promised so much.

Graham Rix's penalty kick is saved against Valencia and The Gunners lose their second Cup Final in five days.

CLUES ACROSS

1) Scottish Premier Division club who won the European Cup in 1967. (6)
7) Books for keeping your soccer photos in. (6)
10) Chris – , Spurs defender. (7)
12) – Bennett, Coventry City midfielder. (4)
13) & 26) Ground of Shrewsbury Town. (3)
14) Surname of Norwich City keeper. (4)
16) To go through on one's own would he a " – run". (4)
17) & 48 Down) Bury's ground. (4)
18) Nickname of Peterborough United. (4)
19) With 59. Non-scoring position. (3)
21) Surname of West Ham midfielder. (4)
23) The World Cup Finals are held every four – . (5)
25) Gradually loses playing power or determination. (5)
29) ---THAM CRESCENT; York City ground. (3)
31) CR--- ALEXAND-A. (4)
33) – Finney was twice "Footballer of the Year" (1954 & 1957). (3)
34) Nigel – , Nottingham Forest striker. (6)
36) See 13. (6)
37) Protection for a player's leg. (3)

38) Eoin Hand was their manager. (4)
41) Part of the pitch where the goal is! (3)
42) It takes two to make a match! (5)
44) Ian – , Q.P.R. defender. (5)
49) Liverpool beat A.S. – in the 1984 European Cup Final (on penalties). (4)
50) First three letters of the club from Goodison Park. (3)
52) It could be the "goal" one or "penalty" one, for instance. (4)
53) The 4th, 2nd, 7th & 3rd letters of ST. MIRREN. (4)
54) Abbreviation of county of club from Manor Ground. (4)
55) – Snodin, Sheffield Wednesday defender. (4)
57) If Clyde, Aberdeen & Rangers give "CAR"; what will Aldershot, Stoke & Plymouth give? (3)
59) With 19. (4)
61) Linz is a club in this country. (7)
62) Another type of light, open footwear. (6)
63) The 9th, 14th, 8th, 11th, 5th & 1st letters of ROTHERHAM UNITED. (6)

CLUES DOWN

2) ROMEO ZOND--V-N of Ipswich Town. (3)
3) – – ground of Halifax. (3 & 4)
4) Bobby Campbell is their manager. (7)
5) KEVIN ST---LES; Port Vale defender. (3)
6) GREE--- ROAD, ground of club in Clue 31 Across. (3)
7) – Road, Liverpool's home. (7)
8) Steve – , Norwich City player. (7)
9) RUSSELL OS---, Leicester City defender. (3)
11) Each – of the game is forty-five minutes in duration. (4)
12) – tests are carried out on all players in the World Cup Finals. (4)
15) WAY-E F-R--AY; Q.P.R. winger. (4)
19) A river required to complete STENH----MUIR. (4)
20) East – , Scottish club. (4)
22) Nearby . . . like ones closest club or pub! (5)
24) Avoid or dodge. (5)
26) P-UL -A-SEY; Leicester City skipper. (3)
27) The 9th, 10th, 2nd, 7th & 6th letters of MANCHESTER CITY. (5)

28) See 47. (5)
30) – Trafford; ground of Manchester United. (3)
32) JOHN ---K, Ipswich. (3)
33) Digit of the foot. (3)
35) If Alloa, Swindon & Derby give "ANY"; what will Raith, Rochdale & Fulham give? (3)
39) CARL---- UNITED. (4)
40) ----LEY PARK: ground of Stockport County. (4)
42) Took part in practice to improve performance. (7)
43) "The Gunners". (7)
45) Fourth Division club from the Racecourse Ground. (7)
46) They play at the Vetch Field. (7)
47) & 28) Coventry defender. (4)
48) See 17 Across. (4)
51) Upper sporting garment. (4)
56) DAVID O'---RY, defender for 43. (4)
57) ---TON GATE; ground of Bristol City. (3)
58) JOHN HUM-H-E, Charlton Athletic defender. (3)
60) --ND-E UNITED (Scottish Premier Division). (3)

QPR winger (Q. 15)

ANSWERS ON PAGE 121

WEIR WARNS OLD FIRM

'Hibs set for glory'

THE one who got away aims to help fallen giants Hibs become one of Scottish football's big guns again.

Little Mickey Weir may be the smallest footballer in Scotland but he has made a king-size contribution at Easter Road.

He's in his second spell with the club he supported as a kid after what he thought would be a dream move into the English big time turned sour.

Weir became homesick during a four-month stay at Luton and jumped at the chance to return to Edinburgh for the same £250,000 fee that had taken him to Kenilworth Road.

"I went to Luton full of hope and desperate to do well," he reflects, "but things simply didn't work out for me.

"When Hibs offered to take me back I jumped at the chance. It was too good an opportunity to miss. I just couldn't settle at Luton."

The diminutive midfield man is now playing a key role in helping Hibs re-establish themselves among the elite of Scottish football – and already the signs are very encouraging.

A boardroom takeover enabled Easter Road boss Alex Miller to splash out on new faces, among them Scotland goalkeeper Andy Goram from Oldham and former West Ham utility player Neil Orr.

Target

Hibs' ambition for the future also enabled them to hold on to Scotland youngster John Collins, the left-sided midfield player whose prize performances made him a target for a host of top English outfits.

"When John agreed to stay for a further two years it showed the club really meant business," Weir points out.

"Everyone at Easter Road is determined to see us up there alongside Rangers and Celtic making a serious challenge for the major honours.

"Last season we were a bit inconsistent or we might have qualified for Europe.

"We showed we are progressing along the right lines and finished just four points adrift of Dundee United in fifth place.

"From a personal point of view I'm just delighted to be playing a part. I thought it was in the best interests of my career to join Luton at the time, but I soon realised there's nothing Scottish football can learn from the English League."

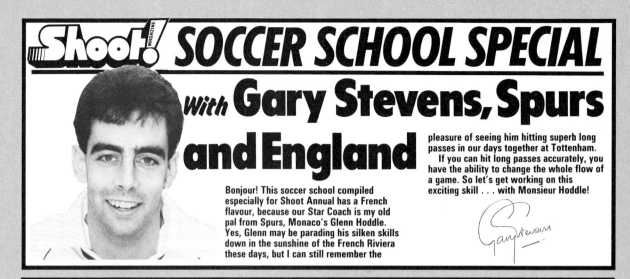

Shoot! SOCCER SCHOOL SPECIAL

with Gary Stevens, Spurs and England

Bonjour! This soccer school compiled especially for Shoot Annual has a French flavour, because our Star Coach is my old pal from Spurs, Monaco's Glenn Hoddle. Yes, Glenn may be parading his silken skills down in the sunshine of the French Riviera these days, but I can still remember the pleasure of seeing him hitting superb long passes in our days together at Tottenham.

If you can hit long passes accurately, you have the ability to change the whole flow of a game. So let's get working on this exciting skill . . . with Monsieur Hoddle!

Gary Stevens

LONG PASSING

A. THE LONG PASS. Once you have picked out the team-mate you want to pass to, concentrate on the ball, striking it cleanly with your instep. Note how my eyes are on the ball and my arms keep me nicely balanced.

B. CHIPPING THE BALL. You may sometimes need height rather than power, so practice chipping the ball to a friend. Another member of your squad acts as 'piggy in the middle' trying to intercept your passes.

C. FIRST TIME STRIKE. An accurate early pass can transform a game. Practise this skill in threes. Ask a friend to roll you a short pass. You then hit the ball first time into the path of a team-mate running into space on the wing. Just like Glenn Hoddle!

Star Coach: GLENN HODDLE

❝Hitting long passes is very much part of my game and when a long ball comes off, it is very satisfying. But remember to also look for the simple pass. It might be just as effective. The longer the pass, the greater the chance of it being misplaced or intercepted. Therefore, you have to decide in a split-second, whether that long pass is really on. That judgment comes with experience, but be confident. If you feel you can create a good opening for a team-mate with a long pass . . . go for it!

Practise the skills Gary has shown you above and remember the simple basics of the game. When hitting your pass keep your eyes on the ball and concentrate hard on striking it well. You could set up a great goal for a team-mate . . . and that's a feeling to savour!❞

Gary's Postbag

DEAR GARY
Firstly, may I congratulate you on your coaching school series that has appeared in the world's most exciting sports magazine. Shoot! My problem is that I want to play in goal, but I am only 5ft. 4in. My friends say I should play in midfield. Are they right? Mohammed Omar, Mombasa, Kenya.
Well Mohammed, height is an advantage for 'keepers. But there's an old saying in football, if you're good enough, you're big enough. So work hard on improving your goalkeeping skills and you could prove your friends wrong. Okay? And many thanks for your kind comments.

● Gary has some Allstar Holidays lined up for 1989, here in England. If you would like details send an S.A.E. to Gary Stevens, P.O. Box 123, Eastbourne.

HANDS OFF GABBI

warns Sunderland's boss Denis Smith

Gabbiadini's pace is taking him to the top.

SUNDERLAND manager Denis Smith has thrown a protective curtain round 20-year-old Roker sensation Marco Gabbiadini.

Marco is not for sale at any price — and that's official.

Not since Chester introduced Ian Rush to the big time has a young striker caused more of a stir than Gabbiadini.

Liverpool lead a host of First Division clubs tailing Gabbiadini, whose goal tally last season helped shoot Sunderland back to the Second Division.

Smith's hands-off warning to a host of clubs comes at a time of increasing interest in Marco's goalscoring exploits, which have raised his value from the mere £80,000 Sunderland paid York City to sign him in September 1987 to a cool £300,000.

Born in Nottingham of an Italian father, Marco's ambition is to play for England, a target not beyond his capabilities, according to the Sunderland manager.

Power

"He is sheer power and pace. Only 5ft. 10ins., he gets up high for headers on target — he frightens defenders," says Smith, who has tied Marco to Sunderland on a three-year contract.

"He's a tremendous crowd puller and I have no intention of selling him. He reminds me of Mark Hughes," says Smith, who, as manager of York plucked Marco from schoolboy obscurity to take him to Bootham Crescent on apprentice terms.

Gabbiadini, unspoilt by hero worship and prepared to drive his sponsored car from York to Sunderland for training so that he can live with his parents, sets his sights on a First Division career.

"If I play in the First Division, I'd like to get there with Sunderland," he says.

"We have the resources and I reckon we can make the top flight in the next three years."

Marco's capacity to produce the unexpected has boosted crowd figures at Roker Park. Fed on stories of post-War favourite Len Shackleton's ball skills, Marco's impudent wizardry makes him a folk-hero in the North East.

"I've got the confidence and I've scored regularly. Eric Gates, my partner up front, has given me tremendous help.

"Dave Sexton, the England Under-21 manager, watched me at Preston. My ambition is to play for England. I miss the odd sitter. When I'm as sharp in the box as Gary Lineker and Paolo Rossi, I will be satisfied," says Gabbiadini, who left York Grammer School with seven O-Levels and hoped to go to Loughborough College to study physical education if unsuccessful as a pro footballer.

BEARD

ENGLAND star Peter Beardsley is football's classic rags to riches story.

Rejected by Manchester United, he crossed the Atlantic to forge a career with Vancouver Whitecaps and last season, his dedication paid off when he was signed by Liverpool for £1.9m from Newcastle United.

But how many others from similar soccer backwaters can hope for big-time stardom?

Take Wimbledon midfielder Vinny Jones, for instance. Spurned by Watford as a youngster, he went to non-League Wealdstone and worked as a hod-carrier for a living.

On November 19 1986, he finally realised his ambition to play top class soccer by signing for First Division Wimbledon.

He says: "Obviously I was disappointed to be rejected by Watford, but I still thought I could make it. I did nearly give up, though. I told myself that if I didn't make it by the time I was 22, then that would be it."

He made his First Division debut three days later against Nottingham Forest at the City Ground. And the following week, he hit the jackpot.

Unfashionable Wimbledon humbled mighty Manchester United . . . with Jones scoring the only goal of the game.

He says: "When that goal went in, I nearly fainted. I looked up and saw about 25 of my friends in the crowd. It was amazing.

"I think the way I have been through the non-League treadmill has done me a world of good. It certainly makes me appreciate what I have now," he adds.

Steve Bruce nearly swapped his football boots for a plumber's wrench before his career took off at Gillingham.

"I nearly gave up the game but at the

BELOW: Steve Bruce nearly became a plumber before making the grade at Gillingham.

RIGHT: Vinny Jones has built himself some success at Wimbledon after a spell as a hod carrier.

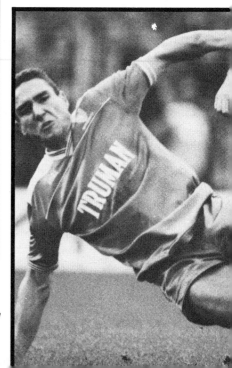

last minute decided to have another crack. Now look at me. I'm playing with internationals at Old Trafford. Incredible," says Bruce.

Mike Newell of Leicester is another player shown the door by a big club as a youngster – this time Liverpool . . . and how he made them pay!

He says: "I could see it coming. I had been training there since I was about 12, but so had a lot of other good kids. It is difficult to choose between them and even the ones who get apprenticeships

don't often make it with Liverpool. Cases like Sammy Lee and Phil Thompson are few and far between.

"It would have been great to have played for one of the top clubs in Europe, but playing in the Third Division for Wigan has provided me with valuable experience. The lower divisions toughen you up and it's far better than playing Central League football."

Mike's magic moment came in the League match against Liverpool at Kenilworth Road in 1986–87, when he

bagged a hat-trick for Luton against the club which broke his heart, and the Reds were humbled 4-1.

"It was sweet to score a hat-trick against Liverpool," he says. "Particularly as they are my home town club."

A third player tipped for future honours is Steve Bull of Wolves. He was an apprentice at West Bromwich Albion, but played only a handful of games for the first team before being sold to Molineux.

He says: "It was disappointing to leave West Brom because I did like it there. It is a good set-up at the Hawthorns.

"It is a different style of play with Wolves in the Third Division; it's much more physical. You do not get as much time on the ball, which is probably a good thing as it improves your speed and awareness.

"I have two years of my contract to run and I would like to be part of the side to bring the glory days back to Molineux. After last season's success I feel we can go on to win promotion to the Second Division within the next two years."

Whether The Dons' man who carried the hod gets the nod from England one day, or jewel Newell continues to be a Scousebuster, or Wolves' starlet hits the Bull's eye in future, only time will tell.

The Liverpool and England superstar is one of several top players rescued from the scrapheap.

Mike Newell scores for Luton against Liverpool in 1986. He was released by The Reds as a youngster.

The hand of God or was it Diego Maradona beats Peter Shilton and sends Argentina on their way to beating England in the 1986 World Cup Finals.

WHAT A P

A gallery of famous

One of the greatest goals ever seen at Wembley as Ricky Villa wins the 1981 FA Cup Final replay with a majestic solo effort against Manchester City in Spurs' 3-2 win.

The Matthews Final as wing wizard Stan enjoys FA Cup Final success in 1953 after inspiring Blackpool to a 4-3 victory over Bolton.

After 90 minutes gruelling football in the Mexico sun the respect was there to be seen between Pele and Bobby Moore after Brazil had beaten England 1-0 in the 1970 World Cup Finals.

ICTURE!

football photos

There are people running on to the pitch, they think it's all over — it is now as Geoff Hurst completes his hat-trick in England's 1966 World Cup Final win over West Germany.

Doc's a

20 famous sayings to make you laugh

EVEN though he's turned his back on the managerial game – this time for good – Tommy Docherty is still one of the sport's great characters. And here SHOOT pays tribute to the former Chelsea, Aston Villa, QPR, Manchester United, Rotherham, Preston and Scotland (to name a few) boss, as we recall some of the famous quotes which have made The Doc a legend in his own lunch time.

1 I talk a lot. On any subject. Which is always football.

2 There's a hell of a lot of politics in football. I don't think Henry Kissinger would last 48 hours at Old Trafford.

3 It's a rat race – and the rats are winning.

4 I've been in more courts than Bjorn Borg.

5 Canon League? Some teams are so negative they could be sponsored by Kodak.

6 When one door opens another smashes you in the face.

7 The Villa chairman Doug Ellis said he was right behind me. I told him I'd sooner have him in front of me where I could see him.

8 The ideal board of directors should be made up of three men – two dead and the other dying.

9 Leighton James is very deceptive – he's slower than he looks.

10 On my first day as Scotland manager I had to call off practice after half an hour because nobody could get the ball off Jimmy Johnstone (above).

11 Half a million for Remi Moses? You could get the original Moses and the tablets for that price.

onic

12 Lots of times managers have to be cheats and conmen. We are the biggest hypocrites. We cheat. The only way to survive is by cheating.

13 Preston offered me a handshake of £10,000 to settle amicably. I told them they would have to be more amicable than that.

14 They sacked me as nicely as they could. One of the nicest sackings I've had.

15 Preston? They're one of my old clubs. But then most of them are. I've had more clubs than Jack Nicklaus.

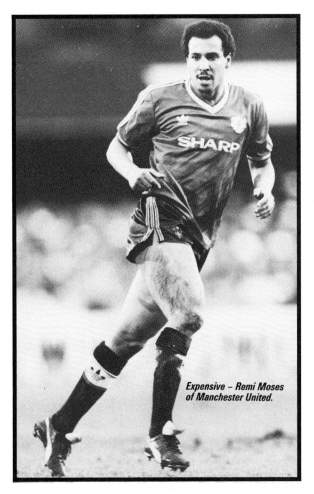

Expensive – Remi Moses of Manchester United.

16 Old Trafford is the only stadium in the world that's absolutely buzzing with atmosphere when it's empty. It's almost like a cathedral.

17 I promised Rotherham I would take them out of the Second Division. I did – into the Third.

18 You could be with Dave Sexton a year and never get to know him.

19 When Doug Ellis told me the Villa board had given me a vote of confidence I said I'd better go home and pack my bags because that was a sure sign I was about to get the bullet.

20 I told the Chelsea chairman he didn't want a coach – he needed a hearse.

CAPTAIN MARVEL

ROY Aitken has completed his 13th season for Glasgow giants Celtic, yet it was anything but unlucky for the midfield mainstay who guided his one and only club to a memorable League and Cup double. His never-say-die attitude and leadership qualities were key factors in the Parkhead club's re-emergence as Scotland's number one side.

MICK'LL MIX IT

RAW-boned striker Mick Harford is a manager's dream – the sort of player you would sooner have fighting for you than against you.

That's why the Luton warhorse not only commands a seven-figure fee when transfer talk is in the air, but the respect of everyone in the game for his all-round ability.

It's fair to say that the much-travelled striker doesn't come into the category of skilfully gifted individuals, but when it comes to honest endeavour there are few better.

Yet while his uncompromising style and rugged appearance mean that Mick can mix it with the toughest defenders, he has shown during his time at Luton that he has a brain to complement his brawn.

For a big man he has an excellent touch, something the club's plastic pitch has encouraged him to develop.

Do you know the mystery man from Dundee United who has sampled First Division action? (see Q. 21).

Trevor Morley won a Fourth Division Championship medal with who? (See Q. 28).

21 Can you identify the Dundee United midfield star above who has experienced First Division action with Coventry?

22 Brazil and which other country have won the World Cup on three occasions since the event was first staged in 1930?

23 Martin Hicks skippered which Second Division side to Wembley Cup glory last season and who were their top flight victims in the Final?

24 Arsenal's midfield star Steve Williams has played in League Cup Finals for two clubs. The Gunners are one but can you name the other?

25 Ally McCoist opened his international goalscoring account for Scotland when he banged in both goals in a victory over who in 1987?

26 Gianluca Vialli, Walter Zenga and Roberto Mancini all starred for which country in the Finals of the 1988 European Championships?

27 What did Everton's Wayne Clarke do last season that kept the name of Leeds United in the Football League record books?

28 Trevor Morley helped which club win the Fourth Division Championship in the

Vinny Jones helped Wimbledon beat Newcastle in last season's FA Cup. Which round? (See Q. 35).

TIME

Continued on page 126

John Hewitt cracked the winner for Aberdeen against who in 1983? (See Q. 36).

1986-87 season before joining Manchester City the following term?

29 Who did West Ham buy from Fulham at the end of last season to score the goals to help keep the London club in the First Division?

30 Is Newcastle's exciting youngster Michael O'Neill a Northern Ireland Republic of Ireland or Scottish international?

31 Who was the manager of Aston Villa when they beat Bayern Munich to win the 1982 European Cup and who scored their winning goal?

32 Steve Foster has skippered two sides in Cup Finals at Wembley. Can you name the teams and the years the matches took place?

33 Which of the following British players have never played abroad for a League club? Trevor Francis, John Barnes, Liam Brady and Brian McClair.

34 Hearts goalkeeper Henry Smith was blamed for conceding two late goals in last season's Scottish Cup Semi-Final defeat by who?

35 Wimbledon hard man Vinny Jones helped his club beat Newcastle on their march to Wembley. Which round did The Dons KO the Geordies?

36 John Hewitt scored the winner for Aberdeen in the 1983 European Cup-Winners' Cup Final when they beat which Spanish side 2-1?

37 Who did David Pleat replace as boss at Leicester City last season?

38 Why was Middlesbrough skipper Tony Mowbray the hero and villain in their FA Cup Fourth Round clash with Everton last season?

39 Against which country did Gordon Strachan score Scotland's only goal of the 1986 World Cup Finals and what was the result?

40 By June 1983 Norman Whiteside had hit the football record books in three categories. Can you remember what his achievements were?

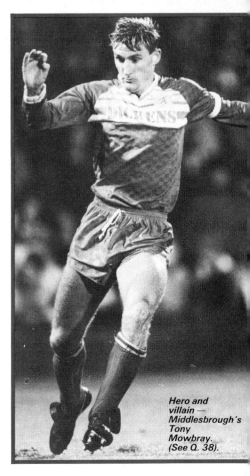

Hero and villain — Middlesbrough's Tony Mowbray. (See Q. 38).

The

wonder of Webb

NOTTINGHAM Forest's midfield mastermind Neil Webb has rarely been out of the news during the most remarkable 12 months of his career.

Rave reviews, speculation stories, contract capers . . . you name them the England international has been at the centre of them.

RAVE REVIEWS – for his commanding performances throughout the season in Brian Clough's young Forest side, not to mention his displays for England since taking over the midfield role of Glenn Hoddle;

SPECULATION STORIES – linking him not only with Italian club Pisa and French giants Bordeaux but with Tottenham and Glasgow Rangers closer to home;

CONTRACT CAPERS – when manager Brian Clough, clearly determined to hang on to his international star, went to great lengths to persuade him to follow the lead of skipper Stuart Pearce and sign a new deal.

With Forest in the hunt for both major honours, losing out to Liverpool in the League and FA Cup, it was quite a season for wonderboy Webb who has developed into a player of true quality since Brian Clough took him under his wing three seasons ago.

His confident display in such distinguished midfield company as Diego Maradona, Michel Platini and Bryan Robson during the Centenary clash between the Football League and the Rest of the World last August provided confirmation of the measure of Webb's progress since his transfer from Portsmouth.

A goal on his full England debut against Turkey a few months later served notice of his arrival on the international scene and since then the praise has been none stop.

Even manager Brian Clough, normally scrooge-like when it comes to dishing out credit to his own players, couldn't speak highly enough of Webb at a time when he was bidding to secure his signature for a further four years.

In his own inimitable style Cloughie said at the time: "I wouldn't be offering him such a contract if I didn't value him so highly."

Forest captain Stuart Pearce is another paid-up member of the Neil Webb fan club and he was naturally delighted when his England colleague pledged his future to the club mid-way through last season.

"Webby is a tremendous player and a valuable asset to the side and we were all delighted when he signed a new contract," says his City Ground skipper.

"He's a bigger name than me and we knew there were bound to be loads of clubs in for him, but by keeping him at Forest we can go on to great things.

"It's not easy for the likes of Forest to compete with the so-called big boys in the transfer market and that's why we must hang on to our top players.

Challenge

"Webby naturally comes into that category because he's such an influential player who can help us challenge the likes of Liverpool and Everton."

Working under outspoken Forest boss Brian Clough for the past three seasons has clearly paid dividends for Webb but, despite signing a new contract only last season, he could be tempted away from the City Ground by the multi-millionaire Italians.

Clough has insisted he will not stand in his way, if the offer is right, but the fortunes of Gordon Cowans and Paul Rideout at Bari should put him off a similar move to another lesser known club like Pisa.

Having made the breakthrough into the England side a move to Italy, or anywhere else on the Continent, could well jeopardise what promises to be a bright and exciting international future.

DIXON'S STORMY START

NATURALLY enough there were more than a few groans of disappointment from Arsenal fans when they discovered, last January, that the Dixon who had been signed by manager George Graham was not Chelsea striker Kerry, but Stoke City full-back Lee.

It took just 90 minutes to dissolve those groans – when Highbury was treated to one of the most impressive debut performances the famous old stadium had ever seen.

Lee Dixon, £350,000 bargain buy, was an absolute revelation on his opening appearance for The Gunners in a 2-1 victory over Luton Town.

Arsenal followers have been used to cheering brilliant attack-minded players in the No. 2 shirt. Even when England star Viv Anderson moved on to Manchester United, they were presented with the blossoming, rich skills of Michael Thomas.

But Dixon has brought a whole new dimension to the position – a blistering pace that has already struck fear into even the cream of First Division opposition.

"I couldn't have wished to join a better club – nor be presented with such a strong challenge to even establish a place in the team," says the 24-year-old.

"I've always thought of my career as a series of challenges and now I aim to respond to the biggest of them all by helping Arsenal win more titles and trophies."

Although it was the 'other Dixon' who manager Graham had tracked for so long at Chelsea, he couldn't be happier now that he landed Lee.

"He was a player I had on my wanted list for some time," reveals the Arsenal boss.

Stoke, of course, were reluctant to let him go because manager Mick Mills, a distinguished ex-England right back himself, said: "You are going to hear a great deal about this lad."

But once promotion became a practical impossibility for Stoke last season, Mills had little option but to accept Arsenal's offer.

Highest regard

Dixon says: "Mick Mills helped me a great deal during my time at Stoke and I will always have the highest regard for him.

"When Arsenal bought me I was quite confident I was ready for the First Division.

"Practically the first thing that happened after I signed was that we went away together to Spain for a week, preparing for a Cup-tie against Everton.

"I wasn't involved in that game, but was still made to feel part of the club. I knew from that week away that I was going to really enjoy my move."

Dixon has earned his place in the soccer sun through a tough apprenticeship in the lower divisions. Manager John Bond gave him only four League games at Burnley before shipping him out to Chester City.

Then it was on to Bury for a spell before a move up to Stoke where he quickly built a reputation as one of the best right backs in the Second Division.

George Graham was suitably impressed by the way Dixon came through the mill. Now he's convinced Lee can aim for the stars at Highbury – and carry on the fine tradition of full-back play of which Arsenal have always been proud.

Lee soon stopped Gunners' groans

SORRY!

COLQUHOUN APOLOGISED FOR HAT-TRICK

HEARTS striker John Colquhoun fired his first-ever Premier Division hat-trick and then apologised to the opposition manager!

The quicksilver striker took the scoring honours in his side's 6-0 thrashing of St. Mirren, a result that piled on the agony for struggling Saints boss Alex Smith.

Explained John: "I owe Alex a lot. It's doubtful whether I'd be where I am today without his support and encouragement.

"I was guided by him during the seven years I spent at Stirling Albion when he was in charge there. He put me on the road to whatever I've done in the game.

"He helped to shape me as a player and I learned my trade under his influence. I'll always be grateful for what he did for me."

Overdrive

Colquhoun left Anfield for Celtic in 1983 but within two years, having failed to establish himself at Parkhead, he was transferred to Hearts where his career really moved into overdrive.

His dazzling displays helped transform the Edinburgh side into genuine title contenders and he soon became recognised as one of the most prolific marksmen in Scotland.

His triple blast at Love Street helped rocket him into the Scotland squad and he made his international debut in the desert sunshine against Saudi Arabia.

John adds: "As a professional, I know there's no room for sentiment out there on the pitch. But what happens off the field is a different matter.

"Obviously, I was delighted to score my first hat-trick for Hearts but at the same time I felt sorry for my old boss. He was going through a sticky patch at the time and was axed soon after.

"Mind you, he's a tremendous character. He put all his troubles behind him to make sure I received the match ball as a souvenir!"

JUST about the only person in Manchester that didn't make a fuss when Brian McClair ended a 20 year hoodoo was Brian McClair.

Frustrated United fans had impatiently waited since the 1960's to see one of their own strikers hit more than 20 goals in the First Division season.

George Best's 28 in 1967–68 was the last haul to top the 20. After that Best, Denis Law, Stuart Pearson, Joe Jordon, Frank Stapleton, Mark Hughes, Peter Davenport and even England's greatest international goalscorer Bobby Charlton all tried in vain to repeat the act before McClair arrived on the Old Trafford scene.

Deadly eye

Born in the suburbs of Glasgow in December 1963, the lad with the pigeon-stepped stride and an eagle's deadly eye in front of goal was signed by United manager Alex Ferguson for £850,000 in 1987.

He had just scored 41 goals in a season for Celtic to take his career total well into three figures after four seasons at Parkhead and two more with Motherwell.

And McClair hardly had time to take off his coat at Old Trafford before being reminded of United's goal hoodoo by just about everyone who could get close enough.

McClair remained as cool as ice about his prospects and pointed out: "People ask if I get fed up talking about this 20 goals thing, but it could be a lot worse.

"They could be asking me what's it like to be on the dole.

"Honestly, nothing rattles me in football, and away from the field I relax either with a round of golf with a few team-mates, playing with my young daughter Siobhan, or by going out with my wife Maureen for a quiet meal.

"I make it a rule never to put myself under extra pressure by setting goalscoring targets.

"I simply go out, get on with the job, do my best and try to score as many as I can.

"It's not a selfish thing, though. The success of the team has always been my priority and that is far more important to me than the number of goals I score, even though the pair often go hand in hand."

McClair's laid-back attitude is perfectly illustrated by his answer to a SHOOT reporter midway through his first season at Old Trafford. He was asked which TV soap opera character he would like to play given a choice. McClair replied: "Clive Gibbons from Neighbours. He's a real layabout."

Yet it would be unfair – not to mention inaccurate – to describe his footballing style as lazy.

He has even been criticised in the past for doing too much work outside the penalty area.

He retorts: "I've played in midfield on occasions in the past and being involved in the build up gives me as much pleasure as getting on the end of a goalscoring opportunity.

Goalscorer

"I've never been a goal-hanger and to tell you the truth I don't regard myself as being a natural goalscorer."

United's army of supporters will gleefully tell you different. It's on McClair's shooting boots that they've pinned their hopes of the Old Trafford club finally prising the League Championship away from Liverpool.

UNITED'S MR. COOL

George Best scored 28 League goals for Manchester United in 1967–68.

FOOTBALL Fun

Move over Aswad the reggae kings of Coventry, Cyrille Regis and Dave Bennett show they can entertain on and off the pitch.

Gary Lineker found a remedy for his goal drought at Barcelona last season. He took to making his own boots.

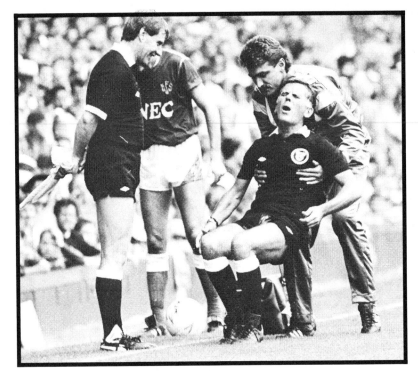

Terry Butcher is shown sporting a natty little tartan number with more cheques than Graeme Souness.

Easy does it. Referee George Tyson has obviously had a close encounter of the painful kind.

Cloughie's message to flying Franz

FRANZ CARR, Nottingham Forest's pace-setting winger, realises he has to work a lot harder if he wants to win full England honours.

He hit the age barrier last season that signalled the end of his regular England Under-21 career, but he's aiming to bring about the improvements that could make him an international star.

There's no doubt that Carr has the kind of searing pace that would make him an eye-catching spectacle on the England scene.

But he knows himself what he has to do to complete the next stage of his exciting development.

Says Carr: "Brian Clough is always on to me about the quality of my final ball but nobody needs to tell me – I know!

"All I can say is that I realise I have to work at it and I honestly feel that I am getting better at producing the pass that leads to more goals.

"Obviously, the main part of my job with Forest is to get the better of my opposing full-back and although I sometimes lose out, I feel as if I do reasonably well on that score.

"But as people keep pointing out to me it's no use going clear time after time

GET IN TOP GEAR!

without there being an end product. At least I am half-way there and it's up to me to work as hard as I can on providing the missing pieces.

"To be honest I don't think I have shown really what I can do in an England shirt yet even though I have played about a dozen games for the Under-21s.

"At Forest we play to a pattern that is aimed at getting the best out of me, but when I go away with England I am expected to do a lot more work behind the ball which gives me less chance for having a go at full-backs.

"But I do appreciate that there is a need for every player to have some defensive awareness and I am making a little bit more of a contribution in that area at Forest.

"The important thing is that I am really enjoying myself.

"As we proved last season, I'm in a side that is encouraged to play good, entertaining football and that suits me down to the ground."

PITTODRIE

CHARLIE NICHOLAS has finally laid the ghost of a Highbury nightmare which had threatened to haunt him for the rest of his career.

The former Celtic and Scotland striker spent four and a half years at Arsenal in an attempt to justify all the hype which surrounded his arrival in England for a £650,000 fee in 1983.

But The Gunners never managed to bring the best out of a man who had been the envy of Europe in his final season with Celtic.

Manager Terry Neill and his successor Don Howe were both sacked by the Highbury board and current boss George Graham could rarely find a place for Charlie in his team.

His contract reached its conclusion in the summer of 1987, but encouraged by his success in the Littlewoods Cup Final defeat of Liverpool a few months earlier, Charlie decided to sign on for another year.

Big mistake

"I now realise that was one of the biggest mistakes of my life," Charlie admits.

"Celtic were interested in taking me back to Parkhead and considering what they have since achieved I wish I'd taken them up on their offer.

"But at the time I believed I still had a future with Arsenal. It wasn't long into the new season before I realised that I was wrong.

"I don't know why George Graham offered me that new contract because I obviously didn't figure in his plans. Maybe he was worried about how the supporters would react if he sold me so soon after I'd scored both goals at Wembley."

Charlie was resigned to seeing out his 12 months in the Arsenal reserve team, so when the then Aberdeen boss Ian Porterfield came in with a £500,000 offer for him last January, he didn't need to be asked twice.

But even that return to Scotland didn't bring about the end of Charlie's troubles as Aberdeen failed to last the course in the Championship race and tumbled out of the Scottish Cup in a twice-replayed Semi-Final with Dundee United.

"I wasn't really looking for any silverware in my first season back in Scotland, but having got so far in the Cup I was bitterly disappointed to go out to United," Charlie admits.

"What made it worse was the knowledge that we'd have faced Celtic in the Final if we'd won.

"My early games for Aberdeen were not good. I knew it would take me a while to recapture my best form after five months in the Arsenal reserve team, but I didn't expect it to take quite so long.

"My confidence had been shaken more than I'd bargained for and in my early games I was passing up a number of shooting opportunities."

Now, however, he can finally see a light at the end of the tunnel.

Hard work

A summer of hard work helped him establish a decent understanding with his Pittodrie team-mates and now he is starting to show his old sharpness.

His aim now is to help The Dons smash the Old Firm domination of the Scottish scene.

"Rangers and Celtic have really come on strong and in the past couple of years after a spell when Aberdeen, Dundee United and Hearts knocked them out of the limelight.

"Rangers are always going to be leading contenders for success because they have such incredible spending power, while my former boss Billy McNeill has done a fabulous job bringing the League and Cup double to Celtic last season.

"But I believe that here at Aberdeen we are in the process of assembling a team which can give them both a run for their money.

Trophy

"I know it will be a very big blow if we don't win at least one trophy this season."

As well as success on the domestic scene, Charlie is also looking to revive his international career after nearly two years out of the Scotland side.

"A lack of goals has been a big problem for Scotland for far too long, and I haven't given up hope that I can still be the man to remedy that situation," he says.

"First, however, I've got to prove to everyone I can still do the business at club level. Aberdeen have thrown me a lifeline and now it's up to me to work extra hard and grab it."

20 things
Mark Law

1 At the age of 14 when Mark was playing for Preston schoolboys, he turned down the chance to join West Ham because he didn't want to move all the way down to London. He signed professional for North End when he was 17 at the time Bobby Charlton was manager.

2 Former Preston coach Nobby Stiles was responsible for converting Mark from a midfielder-cum-winger to a central defender during his early days at Deepdale.

3 Mark had never set foot in the Republic of Ireland before he was called up by his adopted country when he was 18, qualifying for Eire because his grandfather came from Waterford.

4 Former Liverpool team-mate Kevin Macdonald was once sent-off during a Brighton v Leicester match for knocking Mark out with what the Oxford boss describes as "a flying head butt from 20 yards".

5 Before joining Liverpool from Brighton for £900,000 Mark was linked strongly with Arsenal but he refused to go to Highbury for talks. "I thought that if I saw the set-up with the marble halls I would sign straightaway but regret it later."

6 Mark was sent-off for the first time in his career in a pre-season friendly for Brighton just before his transfer to Liverpool, but he didn't tell Anfield boss Bob Paisley about it because he didn't want to jeopardise his dream move.

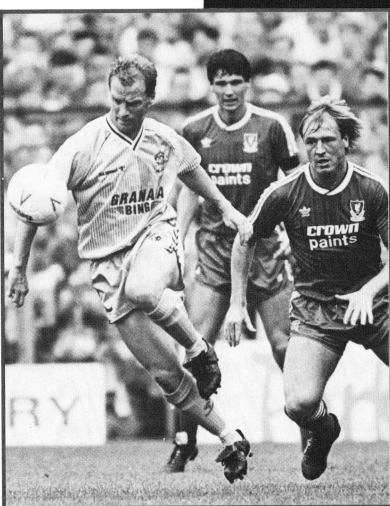

7 Mark received a rollicking from Kenny Dalglish for missing the Scot's first training session as manager of Liverpool. He was still recovering from a shoulder operation but recalls: "I was left in no doubt that Kenny considered I was in the wrong for not turning up."

8 Mark had been keen to get into management long before injury forced his hand and he applied for the post as Eire manager, but Jack Charlton got the job. "I don't think my application was taken too seriously in some quarters."

9 As a player Mark always preferred coming up against big strikers rather than the small, aggressive types and he lists David Speedie (above) as one of the most awkward customers he came across.

10 Former Derby defenders Colin Todd and Roy McFarland had a great influence on Mark when he started out on his career and he says: "Todd was the player I admired most."

11 Mark's all-time international XI would be as follows: Southall, Gerets, Cabrini, Todd, Bossis, Scifo, Souness, Platini, Cruyff, Rush, Elkjaer. Sub: Robson.

12 Mark admits to being a 'Lucozade freak' and as a player regularly got through at least four big bottles a week. His pre-match meal was always chicken.

you didn't know about wrenson

A great player — now Mark hopes to become a top manager after learning his trade at Oxford United.

13 Mark once feared for his life during a flight home from Thailand when the plane was caught in the middle of a thunderstorm with lightning bouncing off the wings.

14 Mark had his four front teeth knocked out by the elbow of a Grimsby player at the beginning of his career with Preston.

15 Mark's second love is cricket and, having played for Preston schoolboys and Lancashire boys, he was offered a place on the groundstaff at Old Trafford when he was 16. He turned it down to concentrate on football.

16 Mark is a placid character but one of the things which annoys him most is reading the comments of former players who now make money out of criticising individuals and the game itself. He names John Bond, Mick Channon and Emlyn Hughes as the biggest culprits.

EMLYN HUGHES

17 While on holiday in Spain, Mark almost paid £400 for the privilege of playing a 60-minute tennis match with former Wimbledon champion Bjorn Borg but passed up the opportunity because there was a massive queue.

18 Mark first ruptured the Achilles tendon which eventually ended his playing career against Wimbledon at Anfield in March, 1987.

19 The injury kept him out for six months, but after a spell at the rehabilitation centre at Lilleshall he felt as good as new and hoped to carry on playing until he was 35.

20 When the injury flared up again last season, Mark knew he would be forced to retire but kept his fears to himself and admits to lying to reporters about the seriousness of the injury.

ARSENAL'S
M1

TONY ADAMS was 17 when he made his League debut for Arsenal against Sunderland at Highbury. In goal was Northern Ireland's 119 cap international Pat Jennings, then 38 years old.

On Adams' left was England full-back Kenny Sansom. At right back was Under-21 international Stewart Robson, now of West Ham. Colin Hill made up the Arsenal defence.

Guess which one of them directed operations, and was quickest to shout words of encouragement to his team-mates?

Adams is, in footballing terms, a Jekyll and Hyde character. Off the field he is softly spoken. On it he'd give the Reverend Paisley a run for his money in the decibel stakes.

"He's not exactly afraid to shout at professionals older and more experienced than himself," says Adams' partner at Highbury, David O'Leary.

"He's a very enthusiastic lad and bawling at people is his way of geeing himself up."

England stars including Peter Shilton, Terry Butcher and Bryan Robson later emulating Moore by leading the senior side.

Adams, from Rainham in Essex, has been a centre-half since he was six, playing for the local Under-9 team.

"All my heroes are centre-halves," he says. "People ask me why I prefer somebody like Argentina's Daniel Passarella to Diego Maradona. I tell them it's because Diego can't tackle.

"My childhood hero was the England centre-half Dave Watson. He was a Manchester City player in the days when I queued at the Wembley turnstiles."

And O'Leary deserves a special mention, as a major influence on Adams' development.

"He's taught me an awful lot, and without him my first few seasons in

GHTY MOUTH

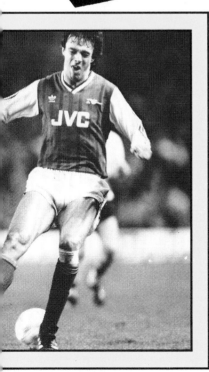

experienced Tony's mighty voice when he won his first senior England cap in a marvellous 4-1 win in Spain in 1987.

Adams admits: "I am mild natured in many ways, but step inside the Arsenal dressing room 15 minutes before a match and you might think you were climbing into the ring with Rambo.

"David O'Leary and I are screaming, winding each other up.

My job

"It's my job to put myself about. I have to get the ball off opponents and if I don't I'm not doing my job properly. But I don't go around kicking people."

Adams' rise in football since his breakthrough in November 1983 has been remarkable. He has been compared to Bobby Moore, one of England's finest defenders, and became the youngest captain in a major Wembley event when he led Arsenal to the Littlewoods Cup Final last season.

Adams has captained England at Schools, Youth and Under-21 levels, and cherishes the dream of one day

football would have been quite nerve-racking.

"The biggest lessson I learned was that every game is hard. I found Garry Thompson difficult to control, and Ian Rush and Cyrille Regis gave me a hard time.

"It was in matches against these fellows that David would mark my man and I'd take his if I was having a hard time."

Enthusiastic

O'Leary adds: "Tony has got the ability to stay at the top for many years. He's very enthusiastic, and is excellent in the air and in the tackle.

"But there's still room for improvement, naturally. His distribution has to improve and, despite all his ranting and raving on the pitch, he's got to learn to say the right thing at the right time.

"The most difficult thing for him now is to stay on top. His rapid rise in the game brought a lot of praise but last season he began to take criticism for the first time.

"It's how he handles that over the next year or so that will determine just how far he can go in the game."

Ambitious Adams hopes it's right to the top.

Arsenal's Eire star David O'Leary (dark shirt) has been a major influence on the development of Tony.

JEEPERS 'KEEPERS

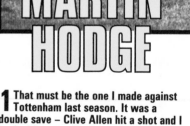

THREE

Hodge at his spectacular best against West Ham last season.

CHRIS TURNER

1 The penalty save I made for Sunderland playing at Tottenham in the 1984 Milk Cup Fourth Round replay, has to be my best. It was also probably my most crucial for we won that match 2-1 at White Hart Lane and went on to reach Wembley for the Final. There were only five minutes remaining when Graham Roberts took the penalty with the score 2-1 to us. Graham hit it with a lot of power but I guessed correctly and got a hand to it to push it away to safety.

2 The goal I conceded to Peter Davenport, when he was playing for Nottingham Forest and I was with Sunderland, at the City Ground, Nottingham, a few seasons back. The ball was pulled back from the by-line and Peter met it with the side of his foot and placed it in the bottom corner of my net. It was cruel because I could do nothing about it; it was expertly placed. Peter knew exactly where it was going to go whereas most strikers just swing a leg and hope to succeed.

3 Several years ago, when I was with Sheffield Wednesday, we met Arsenal in a Cup-tie which went on for five games. I think it was a Third Round FA Cup tie and it became a real marathon. We were in the Third Division at the time while Arsenal had players like Brady and Stapleton. We lost eventually, 2-0 at Leicester, but the five games were all exciting. At one stage, we played them three times in one week. They were all good quality matches and as a tie there cannot have been any better for sustained excitement.

4 You cannot ignore a man like Ian Rush. Yet I seem to have done fairly well against Ian in the matches I've played against him. But the guy who has always given me enormous trouble has been Keith Bertschin, now with Stoke. When I was with Sunderland and he was at Norwich, he always used to score against me; it was uncanny. He was always in the right position to score and as we seemed to draw Norwich quite often in the Cups around that time, it always meant problems for me.

MARTIN HODGE

1 That must be the one I made against Tottenham last season. It was a double save – Clive Allen hit a shot and I pushed it away. But I was on the floor when Chris Waddle came running in to pounce on the loose ball. I had to get up off the floor and push it over the bar, it was instinct which got me there.

2 No doubt about it – the goal I conceded in our 2-2 draw with Coventry last season. It was scored by my opposite number Steve Ogrizovic and was intensely embarrassing to me. Steve took a long clearance kick from the edge of his penalty area and the ball took a wicked bounce. The wind had caught it

MAN. UNITED

SHEFF WEDS.

82

TOP GOALIES UNDER FIRE

1) What is the best save you have ever made
2) What is the cruellest goal ever scored against you
3) What is the most exciting match you have ever played in
4) Who is the most dangerous opponent you have ever faced

3 There cannot have been any more exciting games than the 1987 FA Cup Final against Tottenham. They were overwhelming favourites, yet Coventry managed to take the trophy after an unfortunate Gary Mabbutt own goal gave us a 3-2 victory after extra-time. The game was played in a magnificent spirit and was exciting from the first minute to the last.

4 The ones who are most dangerous are the players who have the speed to get away from defenders. In that category, none is better than Ian Rush. He is just a class player but his speed is phenomenal. He pushes up on your back four and puts the whole defence under real pressure. Suddenly he will sprint for a ball and put a defender under considerable pressure.

STEVE OGRIZOVIC

so much that although I wasn't badly positioned, it caught me out and flew over my head into the net. But before going in, it hit the post and trickled over the line. That just added insult to injury.

3 That titanic Milk Cup-tie we had against Chelsea at Hillsborough in 1984 would be the best. We had drawn 1-1 at Stamford Bridge to force a replay and we led 3-0 in that second match. But Chelsea got it back to 3-3 amid high excitement before they went ahead at 4-3. We equalised to force another replay with the last kick of the match, a penalty by Mel Sterland.

4 Graeme Sharp of Everton would be the man. He is strong in the air and very quick on the ground. Ian Rush got all the plaudits when he was on Merseyside and of course he is still a fine player. But I have always found Sharp to be a real handful for his all-round awareness of situations.

1 The one I made from Kerry Dixon in a League match was probably my best. Kerry had been scoring profusely and he got the ball about eight yards out after a corner. He hit it sweetly, on the half-volley, with great power. But I turned it over the top; a spontaneous save. We lost 1-0 but that reflex save always stood out in my mind.

2 Undoubtedly when I was playing for Liverpool Reserves, I conceded the cruellest goal of my career. It was also the silliest. I was about to throw the ball out to our full-back to re-start the game and I saw their centre-forward starting to close him down. I half stopped my throw but it wasn't enough; the ball rolled out of my arms straight to their centre-forward a few yards away. As I was way out of my goal, he had a big empty net to put the ball into.

COVENTRY

83

Liverp Flops

Players forced to quit Anfield to find success

Left: Dave Watson's career really took off once he left Liverpool.

Right: Ken de Mange has made a great impression at Leeds following his departure from Anfield.

LIFE among the Anfield stars has never been easy for the youngsters who have had to fight their way up through the Liverpool ranks.

With the club still setting a sizzling pace at the top of the big spenders League only a handful are ever going to make the grade with the Merseyside giants.

Last season Gary Ablett triumphed against all odds by becoming the only home-grown talent to play a part in Liverpool's latest season to remember.

Playing alongside such expensive signings as Peter Beardsley (£1.9 million), John Barnes (£900,000) and John Aldridge (£750,000) was a dream come true for the lanky left-back. But he is one of the lucky ones.

Sammy Lee was another local lad who came good, but over the years so many gifted players have not had the chance to emerge from the shadows of the myriad of soccer talent which continues to pour in and out of Anfield.

Among the more successful Liverpool flops are Everton trio Dave Watson, Kevin Sheedy and Alan Harper who found the grass much greener on the other side of Stanley Park.

Watson, of course, took his defensive talents to Norwich before returning to Merseyside to play for the arch rivals. His brother, Alec, is currently staging an Anfield fight similar to the one Dave was

John McGregor (left) was lucky enough to be snapped up by former Liverpool star Graeme Souness who took him to mighty Rangers.

unable to win a few years ago.

Although Alec managed a couple of first team outings last season the chances are that he will soon go the same way as many young hopefuls before him.

Concede defeat

Only last season John McGregor, Brian Mooney, Ken de Mange and Mark Seagraves were all forced to concede defeat in their battle with the stars.

McGregor will no doubt consider himself lucky to have joined a club of similar stature in Scotland, Rangers, while de Mange set off for Leeds, Seagraves for Manchester City and Mooney for Preston.

But of the many players who failed to make an impact in the Red Army few regret their decision to sign for Liverpool in the first place.

Their soccer education at the Anfield academy has stood many of them in good stead throughout their careers with hardly a bad word being uttered about their treatment at one of the world's greatest clubs.

Whether forgotten striker Wayne Harrison, snapped up as a teenager from Oldham for a huge £275,000, will be an exception to the rule only time will tell.

Here are some of the former Liverpool reserves who had to leave Anfield to become hits with other clubs.

Dave Watson (Norwich, Everton)
Kevin Sheedy (Everton)
Frank McGarvey (Celtic, St. Mirren)
Sean Curry (Blackburn)
Tommy Tynan (Sheffield Wednesday, Lincoln, Newport, Rotherham, Plymouth)
John McGregor (Rangers)
Steve Ogrizovic (Shrewsbury, Coventry)
Tony Kelly (Wigan, Stoke, West Brom)
Mike Newell (Wigan, Luton, Leicester)
Mick Halsall (Birmingham, Carlisle, Peterborough)
Alan Harper (Everton)
Bob Bolder (Sunderland, Charlton)
Bob Savage (Wrexham, Stoke, Bournemouth, Bradford, Bolton)
Alex Cribley (Wigan)
Brian Mooney (Preston)
Ken de Mange (Leeds)
Mark Seagraves (Manchester City)

SPECIAL

TOO MUCH SOCCER

SHOOT! puts six stars in the hot seat to answer some serious questions on football and some not-so-heavy ones on themselves.

Questions

1. What was the first game you ever saw?
2. Who is the best manager you have played under – excluding your current boss?
3. Do you prefer Football Focus or Saint and Greavsie?
4. Should there be more or less football on TV, or is it about right?
5. Is there too much football played?
6. What about the play-offs, a good or bad idea? (or for the Scots, is it fair to only relegate one team from the Premier)?
7. Who is your favourite cartoon character?
8. What is your favourite soap opera?
9. Who is/was your favourite pet?
10. What paper do you read?
11. Is the Press a good or bad influence for football?
12. Who are the most important people in football?

ALVIN MARTIN (West Ham United)

1. Liverpool v Atletico Bilbao in the old Fairs Cup in 1968, Liverpool won on the night but lost on the toss of a coin.
2. Hard to choose. All three managers I've played under, Ron Greenwood, Bobby Robson and John Lyall, I rate very highly.
3. Both! Saint and Greavsie is funnier but Football Focus has more action and information.
4. Less, definitely. I've never really been a fan of football on television. Saturday night highlights are all right but not live matches every week.
5. Too much. The majority of players and fans have lost all respect for competitions like the Simod Cup.
6. Good. They create interest right to the end of the season and add a little extra spice.
7. Tom and Jerry. I buy videos of them and pretend they are for the kids. Secretly they are for me as well.
8. Dallas and Dynasty. I was forced to watch them by my wife Maggie and I'm now a big fan.
9. I've a golden retriever called Duke (Maggie chose the name).
10. I stopped getting papers about eight years ago. I wasn't too happy with what they were writing about me. The only time I read them is in training when I might pick one up to keep tabs on which players are moving where. Naturally I enjoy reading SHOOT magazine, as do most of the players.
11. Mostly good. I've only encountered about one per cent of the Press who have treated me badly. Some national writers tend to put things in the papers that they might not believe but know it will sell newspapers.
12. Supporters, they keep you in a job.

ALEX McLEISH (Aberdeen)

1. Rangers v Morton in about 1965. My dad was a Rangers fan so he took me along. I think Rangers won 2-0, but all I really remember was how exciting all the colours and everything were.
2. Alex Ferguson. We were together for about eight years so we got to know each other very well, and we enjoyed a lot of success with Alex.
3. I watch both although I prefer "Saint and Greavsie" because it's more light-hearted.
4. I can't get enough of it! I've had a satellite dish installed so I can watch games from all over Europe. It does get a bit boring watching the same teams all the time, but I like to see as much as I can.
5. Yes. The French and Italians play a lot less domestic football and their international sides are much more successful.
6. Tricky one. I think that you have to give the smaller clubs a chance. They are the bread and butter of the game, but they will always struggle.
7. Foghorn Leghorn. He's brilliant!
8. Knotts Landing, but generally I prefer documentary-type programmes.
9. I've never had anything bigger than a goldfish. I used to badger my dad to get me a dog, but he never did.
10. The Sun. I like to get away from reality for a while every day!
11. Could be good, but they always seem to be trying to make something out of nothing. They should try to put something good into the game instead of knocking it all the time.
12. The fans are by far the most important people — followed by the players! Players should always try to set an example to the fans, and the fans should show their enjoyment of a game. Nothing picks a player up more than a cheerful crowd.

LEE DIXON (Arsenal)

MICK MILLS

1. Manchester United v Wolves many years ago, though I'm actually a City fan.
2. Mick Mills, he taught me so much he was my manager when at Stoke, especially having been a former international full-back.
3. Football Focus. There is more action.
4. There is too little for my liking.
5. I'd like to play every day but there are times when you feel there might be too much, but on the whole I think it is about right.
6. Yes, they keep the interest going for players and fans.
7. Tom and Jerry (is it cheating to choose two?).
8. None in particular at the moment.
9. My dog Shula.
10. The Daily Express. I like the sports coverage and my dad used to have it.
11. In general good. Obviously they provide the game with a lot of publicity but there is such a thing as bad publicity.
12. The spectators, followed by the players.

TOO MUCH SOCCER

On the SPOT SPECIAL

SHOOT! puts six stars in the hot seat to answer some serious questions on football and some not-so-heavy ones on themselves.

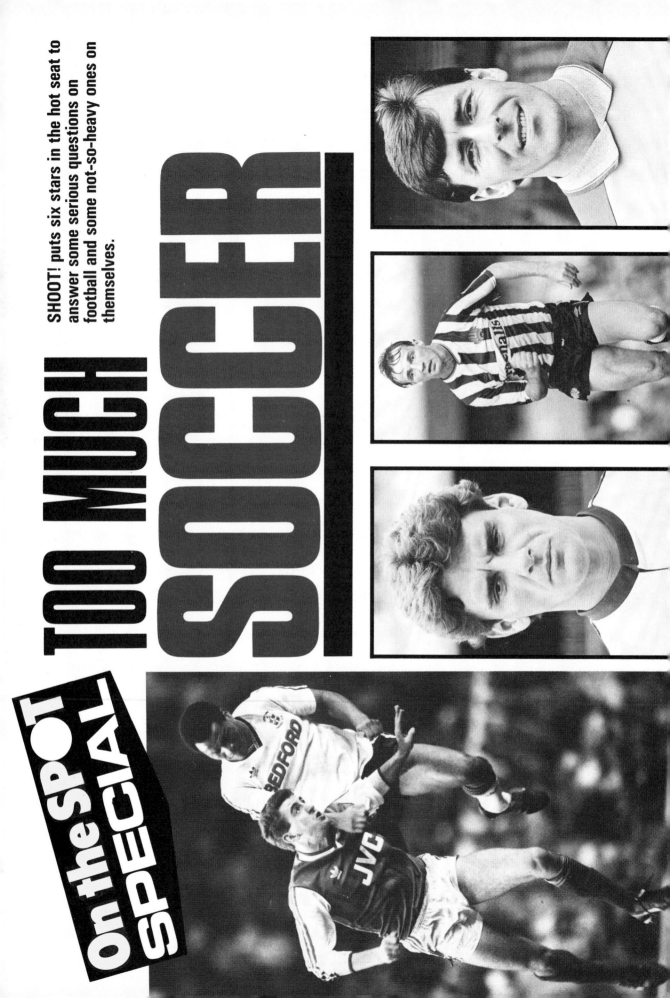

1. What was the first game you ever saw?

2. Who is the best manager you have played under – excluding your current boss?

3. Do you prefer Football Focus or Saint and Greavsie?

4. Should there be more or less football on TV, or is it about right?

5. Is there too much football played?

6. What about the play-offs, a good or bad idea? (or for the Scots, is it fair to only relegate one team from the Premier)?

7. Who is your favourite cartoon character?

8. What is your favourite soap opera?

9. Who is/was your favourite pet?

10. What paper do you read?

11. Is the Press a good or bad influence for football?

12. Who are the most important people in football?

JOHN GREGORY
(Derby County)

1. England 8 Mexico 0. May 10, 1961 at Wembley. Bobby Charlton scored a hat-trick.
2. Terry Venables. I rank my own Derby boss Arthur Cox alongside him, though.
3. Football Focus. It is much better. They have a very professional approach.
4. The television companies have it about right at the moment. I certainly enjoy the 'Live' Sunday afternoon games. I don't think they affect the crowds, either. When Derby played Chelsea in front of the cameras last November we had one of our best crowds of the season at the Baseball Ground. Incidentally we won 2–0.
5. I agree there is too much club football played. I think the quality has deteriorated because of the number of matches, but the play-offs will help to reduce the block of fixtures.
6. They are a good idea. Apart from the reason above, they also serve to maintain interest right up to the end of the season.
7. No one in particular.
8. I don't have one.
9. I don't have any pets. My two kids take up enough of my time.
10. The Daily Express. It is a good family paper and does not sensationalise everything.
11. Generally the Press is good for football. After all, it can be used to the game's advantage in terms of promoting and advertising football. Some people dislike its criticism of the game, but most of the time it is deserved. Last season Derby lost ten consecutive matches at one stage, and there was no way we could complain about being criticised.
12. Without a doubt it is managers. I believe compared to players they are underpaid, especially the top managers.

PAUL GODDARD

1. I think it was Spurs in a European tie against some foreign team. I can't remember who provided the opposition, but I know Spurs won quite comprehensively. It was in the days of Martin Chivers and Alan Gilzean.
2. John Lyall and Tommy Docherty. Very good in very different ways.
3. Saint and Greavsie, it has humour and puts the game in a good light.
4. There's a good balance, but possibly too many live games. I'd like to see some new faces as well.
5. No, not now we are out of Europe, though some of the competitions do not seem worthwhile.
6. Bad one. After 42 games, or however many in the division, a club's final League position should decide what happens to them — not extra matches.
7. Pluto.
8. EastEnders.
9. My dog Hovis, a dane.
10. The Mirror.
11. It is necessary but it can get out of hand. Some articles are not in football's interests.
12. The spectators — they finance football. They may not make any decisions, but without them football's dead.

TOMMY DOCHERTY

PAT BONNER
(Celtic)

1. The first games I remember watching were the Mexico World Cup Finals in 1970 — that was when football really caught my imagination. The first 'live' game would have been at our local League of Ireland side Finn Harps, my first professional one being Leicester v Manchester United when I was at Leicester for a trial.
2. Difficult to say. Johnny Giles, Jack Charlton and Billy McNeill are all good, each with different attributes.
3. Football Focus, they don't give so much stick to Scottish goalkeepers.
4. We don't see as many English games as we used to which is a shame. Most of the 'live' games here are sold out anyway so that's not a problem. I think football needs TV.
5. Yes, especially last season with the European Championships.
6. The bottom of the Premier isn't as good as it should be. Clubs that come up often over-commit themselves financially and struggle for several seasons afterwards. Promoting and relegating only one might mean better-equipped sides coming up.
7. None in particular. It was nice to see characters like Mickey Mouse when we took the kids to Disneyland.
8. My wife watches many of them — I like the Dallas-type fantasy ones.
9. I used to have loads of dogs in Ireland but I don't like keeping them in the city.
10. Daily Record and the Glasgow Evening Times.
11. Depends how it is done, every country is different. The English press seems more international in outlook than the Scottish. The Irish tends to have a go at players who go abroad.
12. Must be the fans.

Kevin Wilson
(Chelsea) v. Derby

NORTHERN Ireland international Kevin Wilson cannot separate two goals which he rates as his best ever.

He says: "The first was for Derby against Luton at the Baseball Ground in January, 1980, and it did well in the 'Goal of the Month' competition on television.

"A long ball was pumped into the box, Dave Swindlehurst got a flick on, and I sent a right-footed overhead kick past Jake Findlay from around the penalty spot area. It was just one of those chances that either come off or miss by a mile. Luckily it worked out right.

"The other goal was particularly special as it helped inflict a rare defeat on Liverpool in the 1985–86 season, when they won the title.

"I was playing for Ipswich at Portman Road, and I actually

TOP S
Six strikers reca
of their careers

started the move myself.

"The ball went to Romeo Zondervan and on to Mark Brennan, who sent a long ball to the far post. Steve Nicol of Liverpool deflected it and it came to me on the angle of the 18-yard box. I chested it down and sent a half-volley past Bruce Grobbelaar into the corner."

There is no doubt about the best goal Wilson has ever seen – Glenn Hoddle's memorable one for Tottenham Hotspur against Manchester United in the 1979–80 League Cup.

He recalls: "It was a free-kick move executed to perfection. The ball was chipped up and Hoddle volleyed it in from a difficult angle. I just hope I score a few like that for Chelsea."

HOTS
the best goals so far...

Graeme Sharp
(Everton) v. Liverpool

GRAEME Sharp remembers his spectacular goal for Everton against arch-rivals Liverpool at Anfield in October 1984 as the best in his career.

Television viewers voted Sharp's effort: "Goal of the Season", and Everton went on to succeed Liverpool as League Champions.

Sharp reflects: "The goal was a little bit special, considering we hadn't beaten Liverpool on their patch since 1970.

"Gary Stevens played a somewhat hopeful ball up-field and I had a

difficult job getting on the end of it. Luckily, I got a good first touch and was able to beat Mark Lawrenson. I saw Bruce Grobbelaar off his line, so I hit it on the volley straight over his head. I must have been 40-yards out!

"Maradona's second against England in Mexico in 1986 must take some beating for the best I've seen. But I recall one that does from a Saturday lunchtime TV preview two seasons ago, scored by Marco Van Basten in a Dutch League game when he was at Ajax.

"When the ball came over from the left Van Basten had his back to goal. He was heavily marked, but turned to hit an over-head kick with the outside of his boot into the top left-hand corner.

"The defence and goalkeeper could do nothing but watch."

John Colquhoun
(Hearts) v. Celtic

JOHN Colquhoun's favourite goal came at the beginning of last season for Hearts against his old club, Celtic.

"We were top at the time and they were second, which made it a crucial game. The goal is especially memorable because I scored from about 25–30 yards – which is at least twice my normal scoring range.

"The goal was one of those shots you know are going in as soon as you strike the ball. It bent a little in the air, which helped to deceive Pat Bonner in goal.

"It is difficult to pick out one particular goal of the ones I have seen. Maradona's against England for Argentina (the second one) and Mark Hughes' incredibly athletic volley for Wales against Spain spring to mind.

"Perhaps the best, though, was Carlos Alberto's for Brazil in the 1970 World Cup Final against Italy. It was a great move, involving several players and ending when Pele rolled the ball into Alberto's path as he came up on the right. He drove the ball in with it barely rising off the ground."

KEVIN DRINKELL regards the goal that upstaged former Liverpool scoring ace Ian Rush as the best in his career.

It came in Norwich's 2-1 defeat of the Reds at Carrow Road in March 1987 after Rush had given Liverpool the lead.

He recalls: "I picked a loose ball up on the edge of the Liverpool box and started off towards the by-line but the Liverpool defenders kept backing off and everything seemed to open up for me.

"Luckily, the ball bobbled nicely and I hit a half-volley into the top left-hand corner for the winner.

"The best goal I have ever seen was Maradona's second against England in the 1986 World Cup Finals. However, one that goes a long way to matching it was a Glenn Hoddle chip for Spurs against Watford in September 1983."

CONTINUED

TOP SHOTS

Ian Wright
(Crystal Palace) v. Plymouth

IAN Wright's most enjoyable goal was the one that completed the first hat-trick of his League career.

It came for Crystal Palace in their 5-1 thrashing of Plymouth at Selhurst Park in early November 1987.

The man Palace discovered playing park football with Greenwich Borough says: "I was standing in the Plymouth penalty area with my back against the goal. Gary Stebbing fed me the ball, I turned, beating two defenders and shot home.

"It was a marvellous feeling to score a hat-trick especially as we won so comfortably as well.

"For the best goal I've ever seen I could pick any of a dozen scored in the 1970 World Cup Finals. One that stands out more than most was Jairzinho's brilliant effort for Brazil against Uruguay in the semi-finals.

"Pele started the move with a deft flick to Tostao whose diagonal pass found Jairzinho, who then shrugged off two defensive challenges to shoot into the net."

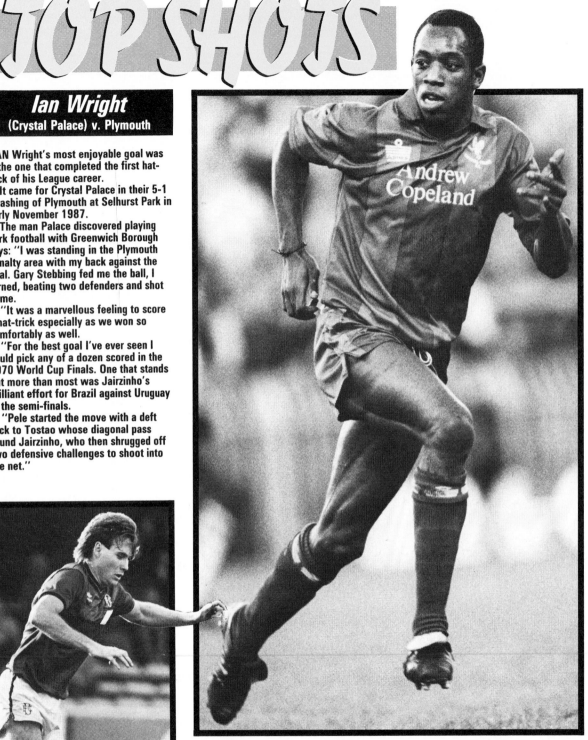

Tommy Coyne
(Dundee) v. Dunfermline

THE Tayside scoring sensation of the 1987/88 season says: "Every goal I score I enjoy although I don't get many spectacular ones.

"But if forced to choose it would be one of the four I scored for Dundee against Dunfermline last season. We won 5-0 and it was a memorable day.

"The goal that started it all came from a good move that ended with our left-back Thomas McKinlay sending over a cross. I made a run to the near post and headed it in from about ten yards out.

"I have seen a few good goals, especially in the 1986 World Cup and one I particularly recall was Josimar's for Brazil against Northern Ireland. It takes something out of the ordinary to beat a 'keeper like Pat Jennings from that range (about 20 yards) and that certainly was."

Rocket-man Lorimer

AS a youngster standing on the Elland Road terraces Gary Pallister's great favourite was Leeds United hot-shot Peter 'Lash' Lorimer.

"Peter packed one of the hardest shots I have ever seen," says Pallister.

"Goalkeepers always knew they had to be on their guard the moment he settled on the ball, because he could score from very long distances.

"Unfortunately I have never played against, or even met him, but Eddie Gray, another member of that great Leeds side, was on the coaching staff at Ayresome Park a couple of years ago and he would tell me some great stories about Peter.

"My other great hero was John Hickton, a striker with my home town club Middlesbrough."

GARY PALLISTER
Middlesbrough

MYH

Four of today's highly-rated youngsters

NEIL ADAMS
Everton

Quick-silver Coppell

NEIL ADAMS' schoolboy footballing hero was former Manchester United and England winger Steve Coppell, now boss of Second Division Crystal Palace.

"I was a big Reds fan when I was a teenager and always wanted to be a winger," says the midfielder.

"I hardly ever missed a game at Old Trafford and would study Coppell's movements carefully and see how he operates.

"My only regret so far is that I've actually never had the pleasure of meeting him, even though I played against his Palace team when I was at Stoke before I joined Everton.

"His views on the game in general are very good and he has done very well since becoming a manager."

PAUL MOULDEN
Man...

Fabulous Francis

AS a youngster, Paul Moulden was too busy playing football to have many heroes among the professionals – but that soon changed when he joined Manchester City on schoolboy forms.

"Trevor Francis was at City then and he was brilliant. He had tremendous skills. I was able to train with him a few times.

"Unfortunately, once he went abroad it was difficult to see him, even on the television. Ironically there were rumours at the beginning of last season that he might be coming to Maine Road. It would have been nice to play alongside him.

"When I began playing in City's first team, Sammy McIlroy and Tony Grealish were a great help and a good influence," adds Moulden.

ERO

reveal the players they most admired.

Courageous Brooking

FROM as early as David Rocastle can remember, former West Ham and England midfield genius Trevor Brooking was the one player he admired most.

"I always learned something new when I looked at the way Brooking played. He was so calm on the ball and was never frightened or intimidated by anyone.

"I didn't ever play against him because, when I joined Arsenal as an apprentice in 1984, he had already played his last game as a professional.

"That is a shame because the game in England could do with more players like Brooking – players that can slow the game down and turn on the style."

Rocastle also has huge respect for Kenny Sansom, who used to line-up in the Crystal Palace side he supported as a boy.

DAVID ROCASTLE
Arsenal

COLIN CLARKE

SOUTHAMPTON

LIVERPOOL striker John Aldridge had more reasons than most to celebrate the Football League's Centenary last summer.

In addition to helping himself to a League Championship winners' medal, the Republic of Ireland international joined an elite band of players who have topped the First Division scoring charts since Preston's John Goodall set the ball rolling 100 years ago.

During the League's existence many famous names have joined the goalscoring roll of honour, but it's unlikely that anyone will ever better the achievement of a certain William Ralph 'Dixie' Dean who struck 60 goals for Everton as they won the Championship in 1928.

Here's a full check on all the First Division's leading scorers since the League was formed in 1888.

Liverpool's John Aldridge joins the goalscoring hall of fame.

HOT SHOTS

Season	Player/Club	Goals
1888/89	John Goodall (Preston)	21
1889/90	Jimmy Ross (Preston)	24
1890/91	Jack Southworth (Blackburn)	26
1891/92	John Campbell (Sunderland)	32
1892/93	John Campbell (Sunderland)	31
1893/94	Jack Southworth (Everton)	27
1894/95	John Campbell (Sunderland)	22
1895/96	Steve Bloomer (Derby)	22
1896/97	Steve Bloomer (Derby)	24
1897/98	Fred Wheldon (Aston Villa)	21
1898/99	Steve Bloomer (Derby)	24
1899/1900	Bill Garratt (Aston Villa)	27
1900/01	Steve Bloomer (Derby)	24
1901/02	James Settle (Everton) Fred Priest (Sheffield Utd)	18
1902/03	Alex Raybould (Liverpool)	21
1903/04	Steve Bloomer (Derby)	20
1904/05	Arthur Brown (Sheffield Utd)	23
1905/06	'Bullet' Jones (Birmingham) Albert Shepherd (Bolton)	26
1906/07	Alec Young (Everton)	30
1907/08	Enoch West (Nott'm Forest)	27
1908/09	Bert Freeman (Everton)	36
1909/10	John Parkinson (Liverpool)	29
1910/11	Albert Shepherd (Newcastle) Harold Hampton (Aston Villa)	25
1911/12	Dave McLean (Sheffield Wed) George Holley (Sunderland)	25
1912/13	Dave McLean (Sheffield Wed)	30
1913/14	George Elliott (Middlesbrough)	31
1914/15	Bobby Parker (Everton)	36
1919/20	Fred Morris (West Brom)	37
1920/21	Joe Smith (Bolton)	38
1921/22	Andy Wilson (Middlesbrough)	31

Season	Player/Club	Goals
1922/23	Charlie Buchan (Sunderland)	30
1923/24	Wilf Chadwick (Everton)	28
1924/25	Fred Roberts (Manchester C)	31
1925/26	Ted Harper (Blackburn)	43
1926/27	Jimmy Trotter (Sheffield Wed)	31
1927/28	Dixie Dean (Everton)	60
1928/29	Dave Halliday (Sunderland)	43
1929/30	Vic Watson (West Ham)	42
1930/31	'Pongo' Waring (Aston Villa)	49
1931/32	Dixie Dean (Everton)	45
1932/33	Jack Bowers (Derby)	35
1933/34	Jack Bowers (Derby)	34
1934/35	Ted Drake (Arsenal)	42
1935/36	Billy Richardson (West Brom)	39
1936/37	Freddie Steele (Stoke)	33
1937/38	Tommy Lawton (Everton)	28
1938/39	Tommy Lawton (Everton)	34
1946/47	Dennis Westcott (Wolves)	37
1947/48	Ron Rooke (Arsenal)	33
1948/49	William Moir (Bolton)	25
1949/50	Dickie Davis (Sunderland)	25
1950/51	Stan Mortensen (Blackpool)	30
1951/52	George Robledo (Newcastle)	33
1952/53	Charlie Wayman (Preston)	24
1953/54	Jim Glazzard (Huddersfield) Johnny Nicholls (West Brom)	29
1954/55	Ronnie Allen (West Brom)	27
1955/56	Nat Lofthouse (Bolton)	33
1956/57	John Charles (Leeds)	38
1957/58	Bobby Smith (Spurs)	36
1958/59	Jimmy Greaves (Chelsea) Bobby Smith (Spurs)	32
1959/60	Dennis Viollet (Man. United)	32
1960/61	Jimmy Greaves (Chelsea)	41

Season	Player/Club	Goals
1961/62	Ray Crawford (Ipswich) Derek Kevan (West Brom)	33
1962/63	Jimmy Greaves (Spurs)	37
1963/64	Jimmy Greaves (Spurs)	35
1964/65	Jimmy Greaves (Spurs) Andy McEvoy (Blackburn)	29
1965/66	Roger Hunt (Liverpool)	30
1966/67	Ron Davies (Southampton)	37
1967/68	George Best (Man. United) Ron Davies (Southampton)	28
1968/69	Jimmy Greaves (Spurs)	27
1969/70	Jeff Astle (West Brom)	25
1970/71	Tony Brown (West Brom)	28
1971/72	Francis Lee (Man. City)	33
1972/73	Bryan Robson (West Ham)	28
1973/74	Mike Channon (Southampton)	21
1974/75	Malcolm Macdonald (Newcastle)	21
1975/76	Ted MacDougall (Norwich)	23
1976/77	Andy Gray (Aston Villa) Malcolm Macdonald (Arsenal)	25
1977/78	Bob Latchford (Everton)	30
1978/79	Frank Worthington (Bolton)	24
1979/80	Phil Boyer (Southampton)	23
1980/81	Steve Archibald (Spurs) Peter Withe (Aston Villa)	20
	Shoot/Adidas Golden Shoe Winners	
1981/82	Kevin Keegan (Southampton)	26
1982/83	Luther Blissett (Watford)	27
1983/84	Ian Rush (Liverpool)	32
1984/85	Kerry Dixon (Chelsea) Gary Lineker (Leicester)	24
1985/86	Gary Lineker (Everton)	30
1986/87	Clive Allen (Spurs)	33
1987/88	John Aldridge (Liverpool)	26

ANF AC

We are the ⭐ Champions

Manager of the year Kenny Dalglish led Liverpool to their second title under his command.

THEY had the manager of the year, the footballer of the year and they were certainly the team of the year.

Liverpool powered to the title with the type of soccer that hasn't been seen in the First Division for years.

IELD ES

Kenny Dalglish's early season buys John Barnes and Peter Beardsley were the stars of the show as the rampaging Reds roared to a record-equalling run of 29 League games from the start of the term before a 1-0 defeat by old rivals Everton stopped them passing Leeds' 1973–74 total.

Many experts agreed with former England star Tom Finney's claim that the team was "the greatest side ever." If only The Reds had turned on the heat in their Cup Final clash with Wimbledon then that verdict would have been echoed around the world.

John Barnes' wing wizardry won him both the Players' Player of the Year and Footballer of the Year awards.

We are the Champions

GREEN

McNeill, in his second term as Celtic boss, presents the Championship trophy to his skipper Roy Aitken.

WITH the threat of great rivals Rangers taking over as Scottish kings, Celtic turned to their favourite son to recapture the Premier League throne last season.

Former skipper Billy McNeill faced the daunting prospect of stopping the Graeme Souness show as the Ibrox manager bought everything that moved in his quest to retain the Championship.

McNeill, having to replace internationals Brian McClair and Mo Johnston, brought in Andy Walker, Joe Miller and Frank McAvennie in a master stroke.

The trio formed a deadly strikeforce scoring 45 goals between them as the Bhoys stormed to the Championship.

Pat Bonner holds aloft the trophy as striking heroes McAvennie and Joe Miller join in the celebrations.

GIANTS

Sunderland old and new as Eric Gates and Marco Gabbiadini celebrate their Third Division success last season.

Ally MacLeod's army are on the march as Ayr United stormed to the Second Division title.

WINNER

We are the Champions

Wolves ran away with the Fourth Division title with the prolific Steve Bull cracking 34 goals.

THERE is nothing like the thrill of winning. Nine months of hard slog through driving rain, strength sapping mud, frozen pitches, and exhausting heat are all worth it for the privileged few who, come early May, are celebrating their Championship success.

From Millwall to Ayr they were rejoicing last

S ALL

season as their idols took centre stage in the English and Scottish Leagues.

For some like Sunderland's young Marco Gabbiadini it was the first taste of success, for others like his team-mate Eric Gates it was perhaps their last moment of glory. But for all players concerned it is a memory they will treasure.

Gerry Collins led Hamilton back to the Premier Division at the first attempt.

LUTON and Spo...

WE'VE WON THE CUP!

Luton's heroes skipper Steve Foster, Andy Dibble and Brian Stein celebrate victory after their 'keeper's penalty save (above) paved the way for glory.

RANGERS

TWO penalty misses had a major bearing on the destiny of last season's Littlewoods and Skol Cup Finals.

Arsenal, 2-1 up against Luton at Wembley through goals from Martin Hayes and Alan Smith looked set for victory when they were awarded a penalty after Mal Donaghy was adjudged to have tripped David Rocastle but Andy Dibble saved superbly from Nigel Winterburn and The Hatters grabbed a dramatic victory with late goals from Brian Stein and Danny Wilson.

In Scotland a Peter Nicholas miss cost Aberdeen victory in a penalty shoot-out after his side were locked with Rangers 3-3 after extra-time.

Peter Nicholas misses the vital spot-kick (below) and Rangers midfielder Ian Durrant sealed The Dons fate by scoring in the shoot-out and was soon celebrating.

WE'VE WON THE CUP!

AGAINST all the odds. Wimbledon, a non-League side 11 years ago, mastered the mighty Liverpool in a dramatic Cup Final at Wembley.

Lawrie Sanchez scored the winner, heading home a Dennis Wise free-kick, but it was giant 'keeper and skipper Dave Beasant who grabbed all the headlines.

Liverpool looked certain to equalise when referee Brian Hill awarded a penalty after Clive Goodyear was adjudged to have tripped John Aldridge. But Beasant flung himself to his left to save Aldridge's spot-kick.

Liverpool were left to reflect on a disallowed Peter Beardsley goal but nobody could deny Wimbledon their day.

WOM

Wimbledon celebrate their first major success after only eleven years in the Football League.

LEFT: Managerial duo Don Howe and Bobby Gould show their delight.
BELOW: Lawrie Sanchez heads the winning goal.

BLEFUL!

WE'VE WON THE CUP!

LEFT: Man of the match – Dave Beasant shows off the Cup after his penalty save denied John Aldridge (right).

DO

WE'VE WON THE CUP!

Roy Aitken gets his hands on Celtic's second trophy of the season after his club's dramatic last minute victory over United (below).

UBLE DIAMONDS

CELTIC clinched the double thanks to a Frank McAvennie double in a last gasp victory over Dundee United in the Scottish Cup Final. United took the lead through Kevin Gallacher but the blond bomber equalised 15 minutes from time and then hit the winner seconds from the end.

The goal that won the double. McAvennie strikes to win the Cup for Celtic.

Top of the class

Back to school with Manchester United and England star *Peter Davenport* . . . an intriguing glimpse at his original report from the summer of 1969.

PETER DAVENPORT

Manchester United and England footballer

Being the youngest of three boys, I couldn't wait to start school because I hated being left at home when my brothers seemed to be enjoying themselves.

As you can see from the report, I seem to have been a bit of a swot in those days, but I've gone right downhill since then!

PS. My mum says she'd be very grateful if you could return the photo and report or she'll come down and sort you out!

GEOFF HURST

CK JONES

BRIAN LABONE

FRANCIS LEE

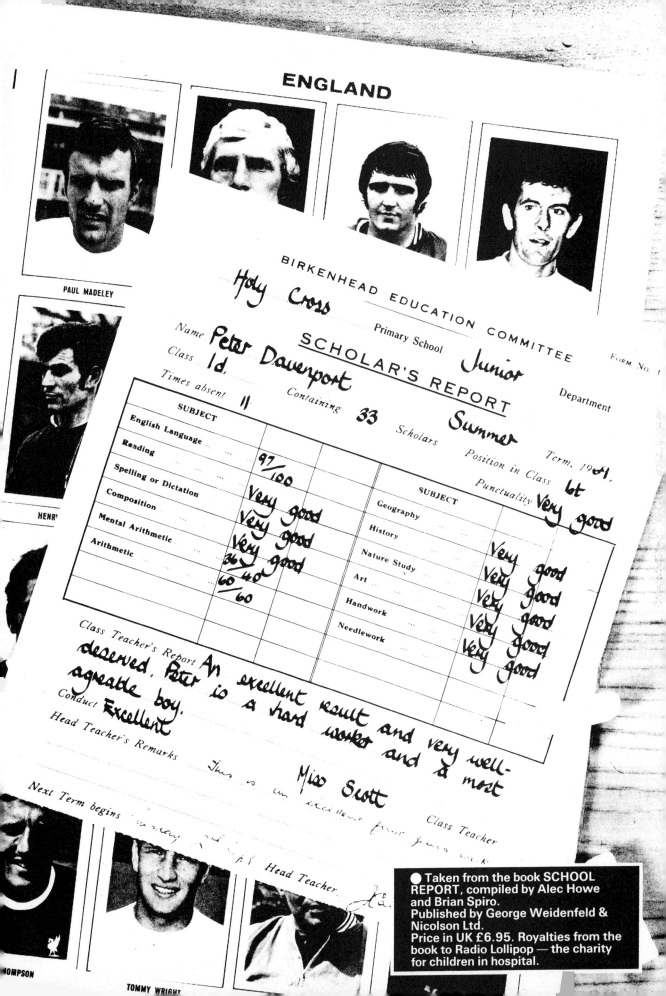

ENGLAND

PAUL MADELEY

HENRY

BIRKENHEAD EDUCATION COMMITTEE

Holy Cross

Primary School

Junior

FORM No.

Name **Peter Davenport**

Department

SCHOLAR'S REPORT

Class **1d.**

Times absent **11**

Containing **33** Scholars

Summer

Term, 1984.

Position in Class **1st**

Punctuality **Very good**

SUBJECT			SUBJECT		
English Language					
Reading		97/100	Geography		
Spelling or Dictation		Very good	History		Very good
Composition		Very good	Nature Study		Very good
Mental Arithmetic		Very good	Art		Very good
Arithmetic		36/40 60/60	Handwork		Very good
			Needlework		Very good Very good

Class Teacher's Report **An excellent result and very well-deserved. Peter is a hard worker and a most agreeable boy.**

Conduct **Excellent**

Miss Scott

Class Teacher

Head Teacher's Remarks This is an excellent report from your work

Next Term begins

Head Teacher

THOMPSON

TOMMY WRIGHT

● Taken from the book SCHOOL REPORT, compiled by Alec Howe and Brian Spiro. Published by George Weidenfeld & Nicolson Ltd. Price in UK £6.95. Royalties from the book to Radio Lollipop — the charity for children in hospital.

BERNIE SLAVEN

Middlesbrough

Family FEUD

Martin Allen aims to outshine his more famous cousins.

CLIVE   **PAUL**

OUT of the shadows into the limelight – that's Martin Allen, QPR's member of football's famous family.

"I'm delighted to be getting a few headlines now, rather than seeing Clive and Paul hogging them."

Martin signed a three-year contract at the end of last year, reward for his consistency and determination to match the success of cousins Clive, at Tottenham, (now Bordeaux) and Paul, also at White Hart Lane.

"I have been given more responsibility over the last year and have grown in confidence. Frankly, the comparisons with Clive and Paul have spurred me on.

"Clive, with his £1 million transfers and Paul, by playing in the West Ham Cup Final side when he was so young, have seemed to dominate the headlines for the Allens. It was always going to be an uphill struggle for me to match their achievements but now I'm confident I'll do so.

Headlines

"I admit I've always been in their shadow. Clive is 27, Paul 25 but even at the start of the season I was still only 22. I accept they have achieved far more than I have, but I think that will change in the next few years; I'm ready to grab some of the headlines!"

There's no way Martin is jealous of his cousins.

"I didn't get into first team football until I was 19 and they were already stars at that age. Paul went to Wembley at 17; it is hard to beat that sort of record.

"Besides, my role isn't as glamorous for my job is to make tackles and stay back, giving the ball to others to do things further forward. Their roles will always be more highlighted."

Why does Martin, himself now an England Under-21 cap, think Rangers can enjoy the sort of success which will put a third member of the young footballing Allens into the headlines?

"In two years, I think QPR will be a real strength in the First Division.

"We were London's top side last season, but give us another year and then we'll have greater strength and experience. Rangers will then be a terrific side."

20 things you DID'NAE

about GRAEME SOUNESS

1. Graeme Souness leads a millionaire's lifestyle, yet he was brought up in a council prefab in Edinburgh.

2. He was born in the Scottish capital on May 6, 1953.

3. Souness' primary school Broomhouse was – still is – reputed to be the toughest in Edinburgh. Tottenham and Scotland legend Dave Mackay was an ex-pupil at his senior school, Carrickvale.

4. Souness was a schoolboy trialist at Celtic, but insists he was a Rangers fan. 'Slim' Jim Baxter was the player he most admired.

5. He signed for Spurs after leaving school, however, in May 1970, and was denied an FA Youth Cup winners' medal by the FA whilst at White Hart Lane as punishment for being sent off in the Final against Coventry.

6. Souness also received a 21 day suspension and a £10 fine for his misdemeanour.

7. When aged 17, he walked out on Spurs, citing his £20 a week wage as one of the reasons. He eventually joined Middlesbrough in January 1973 without ever playing a League match for the Londoners.

8. Souness has always been a bad loser. He used to cheat when playing Monopoly with brother Billy, four years Graeme's senior.

9. Souness' eldest brother Gordon once played for Hearts.

10. He signed for Liverpool in January 1978 and, whilst playing for them, Souness played himself in an episode of the award-winning TV serial 'Boys from the Blackstuff' and, according to its writer Alan Bleasdale, could have made the grade as an actor. Said Bleasdale: "Every nuisance and mood of the script brought exactly the right response from Souness."

11. Souness is the original Champagne Charlie – it was a nickname he earned during his Anfield days. His drinks bill at his Liverpool hotel for the first two weeks of his career on Merseyside totalled £200.

12. The club refused to foot the bill, which was marked down as 'lemonade and orange juice.'

13. His favourite meal is oysters natural followed by grilled lobster, washed down with a bottle of the best Sancerre.

14. Souness succeeded Phil Thompson as Liverpool captain (Thompson refused to speak to him after that), and his taste for the good life prompted the following comment from the-then boss Bob Paisley: "He's got so much class he'll probably toss up with a gold American Express card."

15. Souness' wife Danielle (he calls her Danny) is the daughter of a Merseyside chainstore owner who sold his Army & Navy business for £22 million, set up a £750,000 trust fund for her, and went to live in Spain as a tax exile in 1980.

16. Souness left Liverpool in 1984 for Italians Sampdoria after winning five League Championship, four League Cup and three European Cup Winners' medals with The Reds.

17. He joined Trevor Francis in the big-money League at Genoa, and earned £300,000 during his two years abroad.

18. Rangers had to pay Sampdoria £300,000 to take Souness to Glasgow to become the club's player-manager a year before his contract expired, in the summer of 1986.

19. His annual earnings at Rangers are £120,000.

20. Souness's Rangers career started badly – he was sent off on his Premier Division debut against Hibs, but then guiding the club to Skol Cup and League title triumphs in his first season. Last season the club lifted the Skol Cup again, but surrendered the title to arch-rivals Celtic.

KEN

TREVOR FRANCIS

CRANSON EXPLODES

WHEN Ian Cranson joined Sheffield Wednesday he was warned: "Beware of the training!"

But the powerful defender, who cost The Owls £475,000 from Ipswich in a pre-deadline move last season, soon discovered there was no need for concern.

"I'm not renowned for being one of the best trainers," he laughs, "and when I moved to Hillsborough a few people reckoned I was in for a tough time of it.

"I was given the impression that the schedules laid down by manager Howard Wilkinson would be really punishing and I had visions of me really suffering.

"But I'm delighted to say I coped without any problems. The training isn't easy, of course, but I wouldn't want it to be."

Cranson, who spent almost eight years at Portman Road, was also surprised at the way Wednesday integrated youth and reserve players with the senior squad.

"I'd been used to a system at Ipswich where there were three definite categories," he adds, "but it's a much better idea to put the youngsters in with the established pros.

"It's a situation in which the kids mature far quicker because they're keen to match the older lads wherever possible. And the first team players enjoy the responsibility of

'Gary Megson and Mark Chamberlain are two of the most skilful players around'

helping the kids.''

Cranson, a former England Under-21 cap, soon exploded another myth after arriving at Hillsborough. ''I'd heard it said Wednesday favoured the long ball game and played very little football,'' he explains.

''But I soon realised it was a reputation we didn't deserve. We had some good results in my first few games for the club and we played some terrific stuff.

''Lads like Mark Proctor, Gary

Megson and Siggi Jonsson have plenty of skill in midfield, Mark Chamberlain is an exciting winger and at the back we have one of the best full-backs in the game in big Mel Sterland.

''Last season wasn't one of the club's most memorable, thanks mainly to a terrible start and a long injury list. But at least there was more consistency during the second half of the campaign, a very encouraging sign.

''To be brutally frank, I wouldn't be here if I didn't see a bright future.''

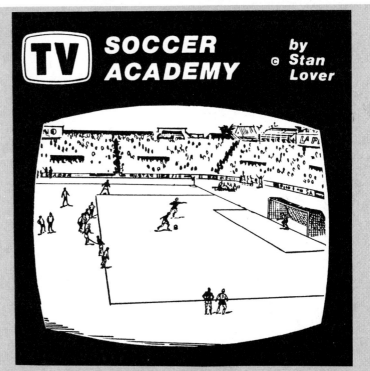

TV SOCCER ACADEMY
by © Stan Lover

PENALTY! TV close-ups will show the reactions of players and fans to the drama of a penalty kick. Some will not be able to watch, others wait with hope or despair as the players are organised into their positions.

The ball is placed carefully on the penalty spot. The goalkeeper must stay on his line until the ball is kicked. Other players must remain outside the penalty area at least 10 yards from the ball.

The whistle sounds, the kicker advances. Watch now the duel between kicker and goalkeeper. Which direction will the ball go? Will the 'keeper guess correctly and make a fine save? Or, will he go the wrong way and be stranded as the ball rolls into the other corner of the goal?

Will the kicker miss the goal or put the ball tamely into the goalkeeper's hands?

There is plenty to see at a penalty kick. Just one can decide the whole match.

If the 'keeper runs forward before the ball is kicked, and it goes into the goal, what is the correct action? Answer below.

The goalkeeper's action will be ignored and a goal will be awarded.

CHRIS Waddle is a born entertainer – whether it be on the field of football or in the field of music. Nicknamed 'Wiggly' because of the way he twists and turns past opposing full-backs with considerable ease, Waddle has developed into one of football's crowd pleasers ever since bursting onto the League scene with Newcastle.

At St. James' Waddle learned his trade with Peter Beardsley alongside the inspirational Kevin Keegan. And his flamboyant skilful style soon won him a £650,000 move to Tottenham and a string of England appearances.

SNAP . . . Waddle, like his pop sidekick and former team-mate Glenn Hoddle, is renowned for relying on instinct. Defenders don't know what to expect, and that's because Chris can turn a game instantly with a flash of genius.

TACKLE . . . His inventive style makes him a natural target when opponents go about killing off a striker's supply. Below, Chris gets the better of a Turkish defender.

POP . . . Glenn and Chris (right) added a famous string to their bow when teaming up to record 'Diamond Lights' which reached number 12 in the charts in 1987.

Tottenham fans certainly miss the dynamic duo. At least we may still see them perform together for England.

SNAP

TACKLE

& POP

GOOD E[

Taylor shake

WHEN Allan Evans eagerly accepted an invitation to join Aston Villa he knew his stay in the Midlands might only last a week.

But the seven-day trial proved so successful that the former Scottish international defender is now celebrating a well-earned Testimonial after more than 11 years of loyal service!

He was an absolute beginner when manager Ron Saunders invited him South in 1977. "I'd qualified as an insurance broker but was working as a store manager in a factory, while playing part-time for Dunfermline," he recalls.

"I remember I was so shattered after just three days that I could hardly stand. Fortunately, the club decided I'd done enough to clinch my transfer and that was that."

Villa forked out £30,000 but he remembers "I was a little bit raw and naive so I had a few disciplinary problems in my first three or four years at Villa but gradually came to terms with the situation."

Evans only missed three games en route to collecting his much-prized Championship medal in 1981 and just 12

ABOVE: "Winning the European Cup wasn't really that difficult."

RIGHT: "I'm delighted I stayed at Villa. I'm playing as well as I've ever done."

120

ANS!
p saved Villa

months later he played a leading role in helping Villa pip German giants Bayern Munich to land the European Cup.

Shortly before their Euro celebrations, manager Ron Saunders had sensationally quit Villa to be replaced by his former assistant, Tony Barton.

"Like everyone else at the club, I believed Ron would be a permanent fixture for a long time to come. That was the only reason I agreed to sign a seven-year contract," Evans points out.

"We were a terrific team, so good that our European Cup win wasn't as difficult as people might imagine. I'm not saying it was easy but I reckon trying to win promotion from the Second Division is a lot harder!"

Evans had a great deal of respect for new boss Barton, a happy-go-lucky type who soon discovered the pressure of life in the Villa Park hot seat.

Eventually, after results went against him and his health suffered, Barton parted company with the club and Graham Turner was lured from Shrewsbury to replace him.

Right attitude

"It was a big jump for Graham to leave a small club like Shrewsbury and no one could say he didn't arrive with the right attitude. But things just didn't work out.

"We'd only played a few games at the start of the 1986–87 season when he was sacked. A 6-0 defeat at Nottingham Forest cost him his job. Myself and most of the players felt we'd let him down.

"His spell at Villa almost destroyed Graham. He seemed to age overnight and I felt very sorry for him."

Billy McNeill arrived from Manchester City with the brief of keeping Villa in the First Division but when he failed he was also sacked, just eight months after taking charge.

Villa then accepted a bid from Southampton for Evans but he decided to stay put, a decision he never regretted when Graham Taylor became the new incumbent of the manager's office.

"I owe a lot to different managers at Villa," adds Evans, "but I would have to put Graham at the very top of the pile.

"His arrival was like a breath of fresh

Graham Taylor

air. He said the club was a shambles and he was spot-on. We needed a good shake-up and he provided it.

"He reorganised every aspect of the club. He's very thorough right down to the smallest detail.

"Graham has taught me more in our short time together than I'd learned in several years.

"He'll get it right with Villa. With a bit of luck, my trophy-winning days at the club aren't over yet!"

QUIZ ANSWERS

KICK-OFF: 1. Republic of Ireland. 2. Port Vale. 3. Crystal Palace and Crewe Alexandra. 4. False. 5. He was suspended. 6. Watford and Hull. 7. Boca Juniors. 8. Sarge. 9. Ian Ferguson. 10. Belgium, Bulgaria, Luxembourg and Scotland. 11. Gillingham. 12. Israel. 13. Nigel Callaghan. 14. They have both scored Cup Final penalties. 15. Brian and Mark Stein. 16. Terry Butcher. 17. Bulgaria. 18. Gary Pallister. 19. Oxford. 20. Joe Royle. HALF-TIME: 21. Davie Bowman. 22. Italy. 23. Reading, Luton. 24. Southampton. 25. Hungary. 26. Italy. 27. He scored the winner against Liverpool that stopped The Reds passing Leeds' unbeaten record run. 28. Northampton. 29. Leroy Rosenior. 30. Northern Ireland. 31. Tony Barton, Peter Withe. 32. Brighton in 1983 and Luton in 1988. 33. Barnes and McClair. 34. Celtic. 35. Fifth Round. 36. Real Madrid. 37. Bryan Hamilton. 38. He scored a last minute equaliser in the replay but his own goal in the second replay gave Everton victory. 39. West Germany, 2-1 to the Germans. 40. He was the youngest player to appear in the World Cup Finals, the youngest player to score in the FA Cup Final and the first player to score in the FA and League Cup Final in the same year. FULL-TIME: 41. Ascoli. 42. Manchester United. 43. Alan Hansen (skipper). 44. a) The Hatters, b) The Hornets, c) The Magpies, d) Terrors. 45. Real Madrid. 46. Steve Mackenzie. 47. Luton. 48. Arsenal. 49. 3-1 to Luton. The first game was abandoned a few minutes from time with United 6-0 up thanks to Denis' six goals. He scored United's goal in the replay. 50. Hearts. 51. Mark Wright and Peter Shilton. 52. Yes. 53. It gave Everton a 1-0 win and the Championship. 54. Wolves. 55. Yes. 56. It was the first time he had played in a trophy winning match. 57. Scored a hat-trick. 58. League Cup. 59. Nantes. 60. Brighton and Southampton.

CROSSWORD ANSWERS

ACROSS: 1) Celtic. 7) Albums. 10) Hughton. 12) Dave. 13) Gay. 14) Gunn. 16) Solo. 17) Gigg. 18) Posh. 19) Off. 21) Ince. 23) Years. 25) Fades. 29) Boo. 31) Ewer. 33) Tom. 34) Clough. 36) Meadow. 37) Pad. 38) Eire. 41) End. 42) Teams. 44) Dawes. 49) Roma. 50) Eve (rton). 52) Area. 53) Item. 54) Oxon. 55) Glyn. 57) Asp (first letters). 59) Side. 61) Austria. 62) Sandal. 63) Meaner. DOWN: 2) Era. 3) The Shay. 4) Chelsea. 5) Egg. 6) Sty. 7) Anfield. 8) Biggins. 9) Man. 11) Half. 12) Dope. 15) Need. 19) Ouse. 20) Fife. 22) Local. 24) Elude. 26) Arm. 27) Erase. 28) Downs. 30) Old. 32) War. 33) Toe. 35) Hem (last letters). 39) Isle. 40) Edge. 42) Trained. 43) Arsenal. 45) Wrexham. 46) Swansea. 47) Greg. 48) Lane. 51) Vest. 56) Lea. 57) Ash. 58) Pry. 60) Due.

On The SPOT

PET

ER REID

EVERTON

What is the worst job you've ever had?
When I was an apprentice at Bolton, we had to sweep the terraces every Monday morning. The only compensation was that you'd find the odd 50p piece to supplement your wages.

Have you added to your dodgy tie collection recently?
Yes. Ever since SHOOT featured my ties, I've had hundreds sent to me by fans from all over the country. And some of them have to be seen to be believed. And I've picked up a few myself from Oxfam shops.

At the SHOOT offices, we get lots of lookalike nominations for you. Do you think you resemble anyone?
They still call me Fred at Goodison because they reckoned I looked like Freddie Starr. But there was no way I could lay claim to that one when Andy Gray arrived because he was a dead ringer for him. Now some of the lads have started calling me Mirandinha, but I'm a bit quicker than him.

Who are your room-mates with Everton and with England?
It's now Dave Watson on both counts. He's not too bad, but being a senior pro I sometimes have to keep on at him to make the tea and tidy the place up. The best room-mate I've ever had was Steve Hodge during the 1986 World Cup Finals. He was unbelievable. He'd turn the lights out, run all my errands – he'd even have made me a hot water bottle if I'd asked.

My collection of ties is quite staggering now.

Did you ever feel you were going to miss out on the big time when you were in the Second Division with Bolton?
Not really. I always try to be positive and even though I'd suffered a lot of injuries, I knew I had the ability and was confident I'd get a chance.

What is the best and worst part of being a coach at Everton?
The worst part is having to put up with the jokes from the rest of the lads, who reckon the only coaching job I'm fit for is driving one. The best part is being able to miss out on some of the more strenuous exercises during training. Kevin Sheedy is definitely not happy about that.

Do you have any plans to go into management?
At the moment I'm just happy to be learning the coaching trade under Colin Harvey and Terry Darracott. I'm not looking forward to the day when I have to hang up my boots and concentrate purely on coaching, but I suppose management is a natural progression from there and maybe one day I will end up as a boss.

What is the worst injury you've suffered during your career?
I tore my knee ligaments – ironically against Everton when I was playing for Bolton – on January 1, 1980 and was out for a year. The match was played on a rock hard pitch and I collided with Everton 'keeper George Wood. The match was abandoned at half-time because conditions were so bad.

What is the best game you have ever played in?
The second-leg of the European Cup-Winners' Cup Semi-Final against Bayern Munich in 1985. The atmosphere that night was something I'll never forget. The crowd willed us to win. And with respect to Rapid Vienna, who we beat in the next match, that was the real Final.

Do you play any other sports?
I play a bit of squash and tennis in the summer to keep in trim. I'm not bad at squash and I'm hopeless at tennis. Adrian Heath was always challenging me to a game, but I've seen him playing and know he's in a different league. I'm a terrible loser and would probably wrap my racquet round his head.

Have you ever scored a spectacular goal?
Don't be silly. Actually, I remember scoring with a left footer from 25 yards against West Ham in 1987. I curled it in first time. The crowd couldn't believe it, but with Liam

Brady and Kevin Sheedy both on the pitch I thought I'd better show them how to do it because they're a bit weak on their left foot.

What are the best and worst countries you've ever visited?

I enjoy travelling, but I don't like flying. Work that one out if you can. I enjoyed playing in Switzerland as a youngster at Bolton. The worst place I've been was Bratislava in Czechoslovakia. It was a very dour place.

If you could have any one player from the current Liverpool team, who would you choose?

Alan Hansen has been brilliant for the last ten years and if he were only 21 again he'd be my choice. I remember playing against him in an Anglo-Scottish Cup tie when he was at Partick and he was brilliant even then. Ian Greaves tried to sign him for Bolton after that game, but then Liverpool came in and snapped him up.

What is your most cherished souvenir from football?

All my England caps are very precious. The most valuable is my first, won for 20 minutes against Mexico. I also hold the PFA's Player of the Year award in very high esteem. It's a massive trophy and the missus keeps trying to hide it because it looks so silly on the mantlepiece, but I keep dragging it out again.

Do you know anyone famous from outside of football?

I know the snooker player Tony Knowles, who is a Bolton lad and we've met quite a few times. I'm also a very good pal of Derek Hatton, who is a mad keen Evertonian. Contrary to the things you read about him in the papers, Derek is a great lad. He just believes in standing up and being counted.

Are you a betting man?

I don't go overboard, but I do like the occasional bet. My biggest win was at York a few years back. I won a right few quid that day, and then had a right few drinks to celebrate.

Have you ever been asked to advertise Grecian 2000?

No. I've had a few comments from the fans, but I'd like to put the record straight and point out that I had grey highlights done in Mexico, but have since let my hair go back to its natural colour – jet black.

Who is the hardest player you've been up against?

Big Sam Allardyce was always a dangerous man to get on the wrong side of in training at Bolton. But I remember playing against West Brom a few years ago and somebody had annoyed Cyrille Regis and he really whacked into me. It was a fair challenge, but by God did he let me have it.

Do you have a fan club?

No. I've been asked if I'd be interested in starting one, but I don't think I've got any fans.

Are you bitter at missing out on the European Cup due to the European ban imposed after Heysel?

I don't look back and I never cry over spilt milk. Something had to be done after Heysel and although it was a disappointment to miss out on the Champions Cup on two occasions, I still believe I can play in the tournament with Everton.

Do you have any unfulfilled ambitions in the game?

You've got to have ambitions or there is no point in playing. My ambition at the moment is to win a third League medal with Everton.

I've had some great years at Goodison, but Liverpool have been doing it for 25 years and my aim is to make Everton just as good. I've said I hate losing, but I love winning just as much.

Is it true that when England made a record last April, the record producers wouldn't let you sing?

Who told you that? They took us into the studios in groups of three to test our voices. I went in with Bryan Robson and Viv Anderson and I managed one line before they threw me out. It's the only time I've had the red card in my life. The only other player who failed the test was Steve McMahon, whose voice is just as flat as mine. Mind you, we were kicking each other at the time.

Liverpool and England star Steve McMahon was also given the red card when recording ''All The Way''.

Some of my Everton team-mates think I look like the Newcastle and Brazilian star Mirandinha but I'm a bit quicker than he is.

WHIZZ KIDS

IMAGINE you had a crystal ball that enabled you to see into the footballing future!

Looking ahead to the 1990's, who are the players poised to climb the ladder of success and put themselves firmly in the international spotlight?

It's a safe bet that several capital kids will figure in Bobby Robson's plans and already the Tottenham trio of Brian Statham, Vince Samways and Paul Moran have impressed at first team level.

Spurs' big rivals, Arsenal, have never been slow to unearth outstanding young talent of their own. First team regulars Paul Davis, Michael Thomas and David Rocastle are all products of the Highbury youth scheme.

Striker Paul Merson, another up-and-coming star to join up at Highbury straight from school, was the subject of a £300,000 offer by Dutch giants Feyenoord long before he had established himself at Highbury.

Liverpool have never been slow to spend, spend, spend in their quest for glory but rubbing

KINGSLEY BLACK

shoulders with the millionaire men of Anfield is a rookie defender with exactly the right pedigree.

Alex Watson's the name, brother of Everton and England star Dave and a genuine Scouser tipped to win a place in the Merseyside machine as it powers into the 90's.

There simply isn't room to list the graduates of Brian Clough's soccer academy at Nottingham Forest. His own son, Nigel, is one of the prize pupils and tiny winger Gary Crosby, a former joiner plucked from non-League Grantham, is progessing along the right lines.

The Second Division may be home to Ipswich for the time being but not so long ago they were in a league of their own when it came to producing stars of the future.

Latest youngster to set Portman Road alight is dashing winger Dalian Atkinson, whose electric pace and amazing shooting ability made life a misery for opposing defenders when he enjoyed an extended run last season.

Wonder winger

East Anglia's other big guns, Norwich City, have discovered their own wonder winger in Ruel Fox and Watford's relegation cloud could have a silver lining in the shape of teenager Rod Thomas, who has already thrilled a Wembley audience as a member of the England schoolboys' side.

Down at Southampton, they're raving about young Alan Shearer who quickly earned a professional contract after demolishing Arsenal with a hat-trick on his senior debut.

Also at The Dell, Guernsey-born Matthew Le Tissier has impressed and Rodney Wallace, whose first goal for the club was at Anfield, looks like following in the footsteps of brother Danny, an England cap.

Northern Ireland boss Billy Bingham won the international tug of war for the services of Kingsley Black, Luton's Littlewoods Cup hero, and Manchester United stunned football with their swoop to sign YTS boy Lee Sharpe from Torquay United.

ALEX WATSON

Do you know Martin Keown's previous club? (See Q. 48).

FULL QU

46 Which Charlton midfielder scored a superb 25-yard goal for Manchester City in the 1981 FA Cup Final?

47 Has Luton's experienced Northern Ireland international Mal Donaghy played for any other League club?

48 Aston Villa central defender Martin Keown joined the club from Arsenal, Chelsea or Nottingham Forest?

49 Denis Law once scored seven goals for Manchester United against Luton in a FA Cup tie but still finished on the losing side. What was the score?

50 Neil Berry, Wayne Foster and John Colquhoun all play for which Scottish Premier League club?

51 Two senior England internationals joined Derby County at the beginning of last season. Can you identify the defensive pair?

52 Has Arsenal's Paul Davis represented England at Under-21 level during his career?

41 Which Italian League club did midfielder Liam Brady leave to join West Ham in 1987?

42 Do you know the First Division side that appeared in the FA Cup Final five times between 1976 and '85?

43 Stuart Pearce is Nottingham Forest's, Terry Butcher is Rangers' but who is Liverpool's?

44 What are the nicknames of the following clubs? a) Luton. b) Watford. c) Newcastle. d) Dundee United?

45 Which Spanish League club does Mexican superstar striker Hugo Sanchez play for?

Liam Brady joined West Ham from where? (See Q. 41).

Paul Davis (See Q. 52).

Published by IPC Magazines Ltd., King's Reach Tower, Stamford Street, London SE1 9LS. Sole agents for Australia and New Zealand: Gordon & Gotch Ltd. South Africa: Central News Agency. Printed by Purnell Books Publications Ltd., Bristol. Reproduction by Andover Repro, Andover, Hants.